The Art of Winging It

What's the Worst That Could Happen?

DR. KAUSHIK SRIDHAR

INDIA · SINGAPORE · MALAYSIA

ISBN

Hardcase 979-8-88869-632-3
Paperback 979-8-88704-357-9

Contents

Foreword

I'm tired of picking up books that tell you to simply think positive, love yourself and be a good person without telling you how to become those things. Finally, we have a book that guides you while being packed with honest and insightful perspectives.

Kaushik is one of those rare and down-to-earth writers who has shown his authenticity and true emotion in delivering his thoughts throughout this book.

This book is a must-read for everyone! Starting with a powerful scene, Kaushik then uses his personal stories. I found the content intriguing, but it changed for me once I got to the middle of the book. That's when the author truly shows his wisdom. This book will change the world because it's already changing mine.

As much as it has been written in simple and plain language, the organic and raw emotions that permeate the narrative demonstrate the transformation of the writer himself from being lost to growing comfortable in his own skin and sharing his life wisdom with all readers.

Beautifully written, one can relate to his journey, take the lessons and learnings and implement them in one's life. Soul-stirring and heart-warming, I highly recommend *The Art of Winging It* to anyone who is looking to change their life for the better.

Each lesson I've learned is enriching and important. This book will leave a long-lasting impact on my life, and I recommend it to anyone on the journey of self-growth.

I recommend this book for all walks of life. It has real-life examples that can help any team, sole athlete or organisation perform better. I know I will be a better athlete after reading this book.

The Art of Winging It showcases a mental roadmap to greatness in the face of adversity. It's a must-read for coaches or athletes striving to build confidence and enhance performance. This book will take your mindset to the next level. If there is one thing I learned over my track and field career, it is the mind that makes the difference. Always. This book is packed with knowledge for any athlete, coach or entrepreneur who wants to step their mindset up to the next level.

This book is the best book to read if you want to change your life for the better. It helps you understand yourself and your emotions and how to work on yourself for positive change. It helps you realise that you have the potential to reach your goals in life. You will learn the importance of self-love and how to respond positively rather than poorly to the negatives of life.

Peter Bol
Australian Olympian

Foreword

How would you cope as a teenager being bullied as school, when school is on another continent from your upbringing and you stand out as the 'other'? Would you have the gumption to take your first full-time working role in a small town in a country you have never visited? Would you have the nerve to directly contact the CEO's of the largest businesses in your country to sell your skills?

Kaushik Sridhar has lived an unusual life that has allowed him to take opportunities many of us would hesitate to take. However Kaushik's willingness to 'wing it' and jump in the deep end, time and again, has given him the self-confidence and the strength to leap ahead in his own development and his own career.

Kaushik's story is not the classic 'boys own' story of the past. It is a modern take on how the circumstances of his upbringing forced Kaushik into many challenging situations, some from which he survived and thrived, some of which were more difficult, that had a profound effect on his life.

To his credit Kaushik has been able to sift through the ups and downs he has experienced to share the lessons he has learnt, lessons that he puts into practice in his everyday life. They are lessons that I feel anyone could use both in their work and in their personal lives. The lessons vary, from prioritizing happiness to being productive. From compartmentalising issues in your life to enjoying the moment.

This book is an intriguing autobiographical story but also a powerful self-advancement tool, useful to anyone in both their working and personal lives.

Geoff Manchester
Co-Founder & Director
Intrepid Travel

Acknowledgements

Dear bullies of my past,

I not only forgive you, but I also thank you.

Thank you for the times you spat in my face. Thank you for humiliating me throughout school. Thank you for holding me down until my arm was broken. Thank you for crushing my passion for tennis. Thank you most for the darkest moments of my life when you made me feel like human trash. Thank you because enduring and overcoming the years of your torture have given me the strength and insight I may not have achieved without it.

I don't know how I could have accomplished what I have so far without your teasing, your isolation, your harassment, your beatings, your torment. It was something I had to go through. It built me in ways unimaginable. I am thankful I was the kid being bullied, and not the bully.

What you have done for me can never be repaid. While I wouldn't wish it on anyone else, I most certainly wouldn't be in the position I am without you.

You taught me about humility. You taught me what it means to care about people and treat others with respect. You taught me the proper way to positively channel my anger. You taught me that being alone doesn't mean you have to be lonely. If your torment was something I had to go through to be where I'm now, then it was all worth it.

You made me a fighter in many ways. By knocking me down, you taught me how to get back up.

You helped me develop great empathy which has made me a kind and thoughtful person. In seeing the terrible part of human nature, I learned to appreciate and foster the positive side of it.

You made me protective of the ones I love. You made me want to help people in many capacities.

I hope you take from your bullying as much as I took from being bullied – to grow and learn from it.

For those who are getting bullied now, hang in there! Your greatness will shine soon and there's so much happiness on the other side!

This book is dedicated to you, the bullies of my past.

Introduction: Everybody Stay Calm!

"You only live once, but if you do it right, once is enough."

– Mae West

When I was 13 years old, I walked away from a plane crash. I had been living with my parents in Nigeria (I was born in India and lived between the two countries, more on that soon), where I'd reached the number one tennis ranking for my age group. It was time to take things to the next level. My parents had received a letter from talent scouts who were recruiting players for an American tennis academy.

At that time, I didn't even know what the hell America was. My dad came to me and said, "Kaushik, you've got this opportunity to go to this place called the United States of America to play a sport that we think you love, and you seem quite good at it. It means you're going to be leaving us, and we don't know when we're going to see you again. Of course, you can come home during Christmas and your summer break, but life's going to be different. What do you think about that?"

To be honest, I didn't know what to think about that. I was an only child. It had always been just the three of us. I was also protected from the outside world; I'd lived a very sheltered existence up to that point. My mother started crying. I just said to my father, "I'm too young to make this decision. What do you want me to do?" and he said, "Take it!" So I took it. From an early age I realized that chances were few and far between, and you need to take them when and where you can. It isn't always easy—in fact, it's often difficult and frightening—but not taking them is far worse. Even if you don't feel ready, sometimes it's best to just take the leap and wing it!

Obviously, I'd never lived away from my parents before. So to soften the blow, we took a trip in advance. Perhaps wisely, my parents planned a visit to Disneyland before heading to Texas to inspect the tennis academy. That way, instead of being all serious and nervous about moving away from home, I could be excited about us seeing Disneyland together. We travelled a lot throughout my childhood, and I always looked forward to our trips as a family.

So we travelled to Disneyland from Nigeria. We went to Florida, spending a few days at Universal Studios, Disneyland—Mum, Dad and I. We had a wonderful time. But the thing that stuck with me from that time in Florida (other than the forthcoming incident) was, oddly enough, when we'd visited a shopping centre near where we were staying. That's because it was my introduction to the opposite sex.

As a kid, I was not good with girls. I mean, who is? But I was very, very shy. I didn't have a single female friend. They were like aliens to me, which is common for many children. But I was scared of them. I didn't realize my potential until that trip to Florida. This is probably when the confidence of, "Oh, I can have a girlfriend!" started to kick in. It was also an early lesson in the way things come to you when you least expect them.

We were coming out of a shopping centre; I was unaware of my surroundings, and I just kept dawdling off on my own. When I turned around, my parents were initially nowhere to be found. When eventually I did find them, I saw that they were talking to two girls, two very cute girls who were clearly about my age. I thought to myself, "What could they possibly be talking to those girls about?"

Soon enough, my dad came over to me and said, "You know what just happened?" I just shrugged my shoulders. He said, "Those two girls said that you're the cutest thing they've ever seen, and that if we lived in Florida, they were going to fight to take you out on a date." Now, if I didn't know what America was, I certainly didn't know what a date was! My parents actually had to explain it to me. I said, "So they found me kind of good-looking?", and they said, "Yes they did. What do you think about that?"

I was dumbfounded for a moment. I didn't know how to process it, but as this fleeting interaction set in to my psyche, I felt a sort of shift in my confidence. I had the first flicker of belief in myself. A belief that was about to be tested in the most harrowing of ways.

The next day we had to fly. We were going directly from Florida to the tennis school in Texas. Of course, I wasn't thinking about tennis at all; I was still thinking about the girls in the car park! I let my parents guide me; we left our accommodation, travelled to the airport, checked in, boarded the plane, found our seats and all the rest of it. Before long we were on our way. We were somewhere over a body of water, which I suppose must have been the Gulf of Mexico, when the plane started to nosedive. Like plummeting; we were going almost straight down. I remember the alarms going off somewhere: *beep, beep, beep, beep, beep*. Within a few moments, the oxygen masks rained down.

I was sitting in between my mum and dad. They were fumbling about trying to fit the mask on me before fitting their own. I looked at my mum and she was crying; she was in hysterics. I looked at my dad. He had tears in his eyes, and he said, "We're going to die. I'm really sorry, but we're going to die." That's not something you're really ready to hear from anyone ever, let alone from your own father. At my age, whatever he said was gospel. He always seemed to know everything. And so I took what he said as fact. This was it. Game over.

And yet, I didn't shed a tear. Not one. I was just sitting there looking around me. Maybe because I was lost for words or couldn't comprehend what the hell was happening. Maybe I wasn't aware that something like a plane crash could even occur.

To be honest, I was thinking to myself, "This is very interesting. I was so comfortable in Nigeria and now we're going to this new place, and we're probably about to die in a plane. This life is about to come to an end, for all three of us. I've just had these girls say they liked me, that I was worth something, and now I am going to die." Believe it or not, I thought that was quite funny, more than anything else.

People were yelling, the flight attendants were beyond worried. It was clear that there was a big problem with one of the engines. There'd been a huge bang. The entire aircraft didn't seem stable; it was listing towards one side. Everything was completely out of control.

I pushed by my dad to look out the window. The deep blue water was coming closer and closer. We were going down, and we were going down fast.

And then, all of a sudden, the plane levelled out. Boom, just like that. God knows how close we were to that water. I remember seeing all the details on its surface. The tiny ripples, the little whitecaps, the shadow cast by the plane. It was so close!

I don't know if it was our lucky day or what, but eventually we saw terra firma and made an emergency landing in Shreveport, Louisiana.

Shreveport, Louisiana. I don't think I'll ever forget the name of that place!

We disembarked. We'd landed in one piece. None of us could quite believe it. Actually, leaving the aircraft was more surreal than the incident itself, in some ways. We were ushered into this dingy little airport in this country town. The pilot's name was Schumacher (perhaps fortuitously echoing the surname of one famous Formula One driver). My dad was more interested in meeting the pilot than celebrating or commiserating with us. He took off, saying, "I need to meet the pilot and thank him!" He's a very social person, my dad, whereas my mum's a bit more of an introvert. I'm a blend of both of them. I would call myself an "extroverted introvert". More on that soon.

But something happened that day, something that has been constant in my life. I was calm, almost serene. I suppose I just knew that things would be all right, that they would work out. I wasn't reacting overtly to what might happen in the future; I was more just allowing things to unfold around me. Unlike my father, I wasn't jumping to conclusions. Things were not looking good, it's true, but we weren't dead yet. And you just never know. Even when things are looking grim, there's always hope that they might turn around and something positive might come up. It's an attitude that has carried me through my life, through some very good times, and also through some very dark times.

It's also an attitude that has helped me to say yes to opportunities that have come my way, some that technically I might not have been ready for—whether because of experience or education—but I took them anyway with openness and curiosity, energy and positivity, and a willingness to learn and draw on my previous experiences and make them transferable across disciplines, industries and companies. I didn't know for sure that I'd be successful from the outset—how could I?—but I've always set myself up for success by going into things with the right attitude. I've worked in a range of different fields, I've played tennis against the best, I've coached children and adults, I've taught across a variety of business courses at university level, I've earned a PhD, I've been a mentor, a public speaker and motivational coach. I have also been a pioneer in the nascent and very important field of Corporate Sustainability with some of the world's biggest companies. For the most part, I haven't planned any of it—I'm not much for five or 10-year plans—but rather just rolled with opportunities as they've arisen. And it hasn't always been beer and skittles. I've been through many tough, scary, bleak times (more on them soon): I've been held at gunpoint, I've survived plane and car crashes, I endured years of schoolyard bullying and isolation, I've learned to cope with academic, sporting and corporate pressures, and I've faced redundancies and had to rebuild time and again. All in the space of 39 years on this planet!

In this book you'll learn about all the hard times, and how they've helped shape my worldview and made me the man I am today. You will also read about my life and learn how and why traditional structures and ways of doing things have never really worked for me. Throughout my life, I've learned how to break away, make sometimes frightening leaps, and forge my own path, often flying by the seat of my pants! It's not always easy to run against the wind. You will encounter resistance. You will have doubts and doubters. You will need an inner resolve, one that can be cultivated and enhanced.

In particular, this book will show you how to:

- Forget about what others think
- Appreciate the true value of your time
- Make full use of your talents and experience across disciplines and industries
- Cultivate, maintain and utilize fulfilling professional relationships
- Attract the eye of potential employers and make *them* chase *you*
- Navigate change
- Seize opportunities
- Be resourceful and inventive
- Operate outside your comfort zone
- Create win-win situations for yourself and your employer
- Negotiate obstacles to carve your own path: prejudices, wealth (or lack of it), education, health
- Cultivate a worldly mindset
- Bounce back after a setback
- Thrive in a crisis
- Walk away when something's not right for you
- Pivot your career

- Face resistance, feedback and criticism
- And value your experiences—especially if they are different!

Having grown up in India, Nigeria, the United States, and now calling Australia home, I have found that when it comes to forging your own path, there are no established rules. You have to make them for yourself. The ideas and insights contained in this book apply to life as well as business. They'll help you to learn how to back yourself and cultivate a mindset that will see you make the most of any situation or opportunity. In developing them, I've learned how to break away from expectations and unhelpful pressures, and found that the only way to fly is by truly winging it!

Finally, I'll leave you with an important note: All of the people's names used in this book (excluding that of my wife Veema's) have been altered in order to protect their privacy and that of their families and friends.

Part One

Childhood

I'm an only child. Growing up I didn't have too many people around me except my parents. And we were nomadic; from my earliest years, we were moving around a lot. I was born in Coimbatore, a little town in South India. It's where my mum is from. My dad, however, is from Salem, which is a good 10 hours away by train.

My parents had an arranged marriage in 1982, and I was born in 1983. It didn't take them long to pop me out! My dad was 30 at the time, my mum was 20. It's a bit of an age gap, but not that uncommon. As soon as I was born, we moved to Hyderabad.

My memories of our brief time in Hyderabad are hazy. As I said, there were not many people around me; it was mainly just my mum because my dad was a salesman, so he'd be travelling all over the countryside. He worked for a chemicals company, but he also he had a side hustle as a wholesaler for chemicals for another company, which meant he wasn't home that much. I didn't have close family or grandparents around because they were all in Tamil Nadu. So perhaps because of that, or because it's just my nature—likely, a bit of both—I was something of an introvert, very quiet. The only time I would really make a fuss is when it was time to eat, being a very picky eater. I'd cry a lot and be incredibly picky around food at that time.

Oddly enough, the only way my mother could get me to eat was to lift me up into the balcony and make me look outside. When I saw people, that's when I would eat. There was something about seeing people and motion that gave me an appetite, that excited me. It was the only time that I'd be quiet and eat. So, you see, I was quite a solitary figure, but I also needed people. Literally, I needed them in order to survive!

Caption: Ready for my evening walk (the only time I was 'social')

Memories of my childhood start coming more into focus when we move from Hyderabad to Nigeria. This happened when I was three years old. The story goes that my dad was a bit of a hothead. He'd quit jobs at the drop of a hat. *Bam*, done. (I see that I'm a bit like that, too! The difference being that I would have a plan regarding where to go next; he'd quit without a thought for where he might land!) But at that stage, I guess he was still figuring out what he wanted to do. Was India really exciting him? He'd just had a child. What did the future look like for us as a family, as a nuclear family?

My parents only ever wanted one child. According to them, they wanted to give everything to that child. Attention, inheritance, the love, affection, everything. As I was growing up, I would always ask them, "Why don't I have a brother? Why don't I have a sister?" And they would say, "You are our eye." It's an Indian expression; when you say, "You're my eye", that means "you're my life". They said to me, "We wanted just one because we were not very wealthy, we didn't know what the future held for us, so we wanted to make sure that we have one, and we can put all our attention behind that one person."

Caption: My two 'eyes'

But there is another side to this story, as I learned recently when I flew back to India to visit my then-very-sick father who was in ICU. He was not looking terribly well at all, and we were worried whether he'd make it. But now, all these years later, I said to them, "You see, now we're suffering because you had one child, and that child is now in Australia, so it's hard to look after you. Whereas if you'd had a second child based in India, it might have been easier."

Now, I don't know if it was the medication talking or what, but my dad revealed that actually they did try to have a second child, but that had ended in a miscarriage. I'm not sure why he'd say that if it wasn't true. Anyway, there was a lot of medication involved. In the end, however, it makes little difference, the result is the same: I'm an only child.

So that was that. It was just me and them. As for Dad quitting jobs left, right and centre, I think he was still finding his feet. He was feeling a bit of a gap in his life, and he thought that moving to another country, being exposed to a more global culture, might be what he'd been looking for. I inherited this from him: lateral thinking. If you can't find what you want in your immediate area, don't be afraid to look further afield. There's a whole world out there, and the chances of finding what you're looking for are actually very good if you cast your net wide enough!

Dad's brother was working in Lagos, but he wasn't happy and wanted to return to India. Which meant that his position would be vacant. At that time, the company his brother was working at wasn't doing too well. It was an electronics company similar to a Samsung or an LG, started by a couple of Indian brothers based in London. They'd tapped into the African market, but they weren't sure what they were trying to sell, didn't have a clear idea of what they were about. So my dad saw an opportunity. I'm not sure exactly what he saw, but he saw something and decided to take a gamble. And it was a gamble because Nigeria was not the most appealing country at the time. But he saw it as an opportunity, and obviously it was harder to find opportunities in those days; they didn't have the platforms we have now, with everything being online and everyone part of a global community. So I think he seized it and took my mum and me.

Mum tells me I cried the entire way from India to Nigeria. I was not that young; I was three years old! But I was just a crier. I used to cry all the time. No doubt I endeared myself to all the passengers on that plane!

But eventually we got to Lagos, and we lived in a little house in a slightly remote suburb called Ilupeju (forever tattooed in my heart!). It was my first time on an international flight, and despite the endless tears, it no doubt ignited a passion inside me, because travel has become something of an addiction for me. To date, I've visited over 40 countries, and if it wasn't for this pandemic, that count would be much higher!

Nigeria: Unfamiliar Territory

I was stepping into very unfamiliar territory. As I've mentioned, I'd had something of a protected upbringing. I was enrolled in the Indian Language School, the only Indian school in Lagos, despite the massive Indian community there. So although we were in a foreign country, I was still surrounded by Indians.

Still, one of the people I was closest to was our first maid, Grace; she was Nigerian. I think she was more my mother than my mum at the time, because she would look after me pretty much all the time. My mum had become a teacher at the Indian Language School, while my dad had started working for the electronics company. Grace would bathe and feed me, and she knew how to make Indian food, so that was a massive bonus. Having left India behind, we wanted to make sure we had something of home with us, and that was the cuisine. We were pretty lucky to have facilities like a maid and a driver, which my father's company provided. It was something of a privileged upbringing, a protected upbringing.

Moving to Lagos wasn't only risky in terms of my father's job prospects, it could also be a dangerous place. At the time there was an informal curfew, and my dad would come home by 5 p.m. I wasn't allowed to go out after 5:30 p.m., and I would wonder, "What's the deal? What's the big problem?" I didn't really comprehend danger and death, kidnapping, murder, and all those sorts of things.

In a way, I grew up with lockdowns! Lagos would go into a metaphoric lockdown at 6 p.m. We couldn't venture out, and I couldn't understand the reason for that. At least, not initially.

One of the first dangerous incidents that I experienced, was when I was about five years old. There were some large trees in front of our house. At night, you could see their shadows like big swaying beings. I would always sleep beside my dad. It went my mum, my dad in the middle, and me. I was not overly affectionate towards my mum. I have absolutely no idea why. I was affectionate with my dad, and he was the one who would give me comfort. Mum was more the disciplinarian; she would be the one who did the whipping if I was misbehaving. But Dad would come home and be kind of the saviour. I often played the emotional trauma card and Dad would take care of it.

I remember one night, I'd just woken up and I saw the trees outside our house moving. Then I saw some other shadows on top of those trees, they were moving too. I wasn't sure what those shadows were, and I was too scared to wake up my parents.

I've always had this thing where I didn't want to disturb people, whether they were taking a nap or sleeping or anything. I would be scared to go to the toilet, I'd be scared to make any noise. I had a fear of disturbing people. I'm not sure where that stemmed from.

The next thing I knew, people crashed into our balcony windows. I heard the windows smashing and four Nigerians entering our house. Mum and Dad woke up in a panic. Suddenly, they had me in a chokehold with a gun to my head. I think they very quickly put two and two together and could see I was an only child. Jackpot for them. They demanded gold and money. They'd come well-prepared; they had a truck outside, which meant they could also take our furniture, fridge, and television. It was all planned, almost rehearsed. This wasn't their first rodeo, that's for sure. As with the plane crash, as with so many seemingly traumatic experiences in my life, I remained perfectly calm. I didn't cry or scream or even freeze. I seem to have a natural ability to remain calm in a crisis. Of course, this is not always the case; when things are overwhelming, I've found that being able to compartmentalize is an essential skill (more on compartmentalizing soon!).

I've thought about that first break-in (it was to be the first of three home invasions), seeing those figures in the trees and not wishing to disturb my parents, not wanting to wake them. This is perhaps my introverted side, but I think also there are deeper explanations for it.

We were not the noisy type of family, and I was often told not to be noisy, to keep quiet. Which meant I had to find ways to occupy myself without ranting and raving. Actually, it was a good lesson, how to keep to myself. Even today my mum says, "You always found a way to keep yourself busy." And that's important, I think, in life as well as business. You need to think for yourself, find things to do, be curious. So that was a good thing; the flipside, however, is not so good; it means you don't wake up your parents when someone's trying to break into your house!

But I always found a way to keep myself busy. I had a train set. I would find ways to entertain myself with spoons, knives and forks. Either playing music or making little formations. I was very tactile as a child, but also it was an inherent thing where I would always find ways to keep myself busy, because my mum and dad had their own things to do, so I needed to find my own thing to do.

Having said that, I loved to go out. I was a bit like a pet dog in that respect; three times per day I'd get myself dressed, put on my boots and go to the front door, demanding to be walked! I don't know if it was just discovering what I would see, whether it would fascinate me. I wasn't sure what I was seeing. Maybe it was the trees, maybe parks, maybe people, buskers or restaurants, but I just needed to go out three times a day. Like the way Mum would get me to eat by lifting me up on the balcony so I could see people going by; I just needed some action.

Soon after arriving in Nigeria, I started to go to kindergarten. That's when the socialization with other people outside my own family commenced for me. Despite my introvert tendencies, I found I was very good at being people's friends. It was something about satisfying other people's needs. I'd find ways to make them happy, and they would instantly call me their friend. I liked that.

Because I hadn't really had a friend until then. And when I saw people together in kindergarten, and I saw their relationships, the smiles and laughter and the fun they were all having, I realized, "I need to make sure that I get people to like me!"

I don't know if it was the way I was programmed, but I would always find a way to get people to connect with me and get close to me pretty quickly I had built a reasonable network, but I wasn't the popular one in the group, I wasn't the most talkative. Still, via my own quiet ways, I would always keep everyone happy.

Despite having relocated to Lagos, my life was still fairly Indian. At the Indian Language School, all my friends were Indian, all the teachers were Indian. I wasn't really interacting with the locals, with the Nigerian population (other than those breaking into our house). That was more or less the environment my parents brought me up in.

My days followed a particular routine. I'd wake up and my parents would shower me, so I was pretty spoiled for a long time, practically until I left for America. Anyway, they'd shower me. And then, in the Indian tradition, they'd put coconut oil on my hair and talcum powder on my face (these were all things I would get bullied for later on in life) and comb my hair in a certain way. They also put a little Vibhuti (a dot, in either red or white) on my forehead. I would then pray to God, pray to the Hindu gods, every morning for 15 minutes. Then I would have my breakfast and later be taken to school by our driver.

A note on the Lagos traffic, a looming feature of my upbringing! It was its own hulking, slothful organism, known somewhat affectionately and resignedly as "the go-slow". In Lagos, one kilometre can take two hours due to traffic. Sometimes I would sit in traffic for two hours just to get to school. You always had to allow for the go-slow; we always had to leave at a certain time. Going in that traffic to school and coming back home in that traffic was a tiring experience. We spent so much of life in the car! Of course, walking was out of the question. Not only because of the distance (school was about ten kilometres away), but also because it wasn't safe.

I spent my time in the car just observing, which I was very good at as a kid. There would be four of us in the car: Mum, Dad, myself and the driver. Dad would be pissed off with the traffic, and he'd constantly be telling the driver, "Switch the lanes!" He was very annoying. Whereas Mum would get quite tense about whether we'd make it to our destination on time; she'd be constantly looking at her watch and sighing. As for me, I would just sit. I knew that I might be late, but it didn't faze me. There were buskers around the car trying to sell stuff, coming and going. There was the noise, the smog and stink of it all. The tension. But I would just sit. I would either zone out or just sit and admire what's happening around me. Again, it was a matter, I think, of putting things in perspective; unconsciously, this was part of my DNA. Things that faze other people just seem not to bother me. Sitting in traffic can make a lot of people angry or tense, but I was cool with it. There was no point in being stressed about it; how would that help the situation? The only person affected by that would have been me. We would eventually get to where we were going. Throughout my life, I've always tried to keep things in perspective and, above all, to keep them simple. There's real beauty and satisfaction in simplicity.

Lesson 1: Keeping a Clear Mind

"Life is really simple, but we insist on making it complicated."

– Confucius

One of our society's biggest problems is that we as individuals are never taught how to live a simple life. We are taught to always want more and complicate things by confusing us with the rubbish mantra of *"more, more, more!"*

A clear mind can lead to a happy life. People must be self-sufficient and happy, tolerant, and magnanimous. Try not to make things overly complicated. If your soul is overloaded, you will complain and worry about others. It is necessary to reduce the load you carry by not clinging to unhelpful memories and unpleasant people. Let things that do not matter be brushed aside.

Four Ways to Lead a Simpler Life

If there is anything worth rushing for, it's rushing toward a slower pace and a simple life. Here are four actionable steps you can implement today to simplify your life:

1. Determine Your Values and Priorities

How do you want to spend your time? When starting your simplifying journey, it's important to get clear about your goals, values, and priorities. Knowing what you value will help you decide what you want to keep in your life and what you can let go of.

Sometimes it's tempting to fill your calendar simply because you don't know how to say "no" (see number two), or you have what the kids call FOMO, or Fear of Missing Out. You sign up for everything because it all sounds good or fun. And maybe it is all good or fun, but when you get serious about your values and goals, you learn to say "no" to even the good stuff that isn't aligned with what matters most.

Knowing your values also keeps you motivated to keep working toward simple living. Values act as your compass to help you stay on track as you are simplifying.

2. Learn the Art of Saying "No" So You Can Say "Yes" to the Simple Pleasures of Slow Living

Simplifying your life requires you to decide what matters most and what you want to prioritize. So naturally, the next step is to learn to say "no" to things that don't line up with your goals. Saying "no" isn't always easy. But with a little practice and the right motivation, it gets easier and helps to define your goals and values even more.

3. For a Simple Life, Slow Down and Practice Gratitude

> *"Gratitude turns what we have into enough."*

> **– Aesop**

Showing gratitude for what we already have is the foundation of simple living. When we slow down and start noticing what we have, appreciating our life for what it is right now, we begin realizing just how little we really need for a happy life.

4. Embrace a Gentler Pace with Slow Living

Lastly, slow down, intentionally. With less on your calendar and fewer possessions to care for, you can begin to embrace a slower pace of life and be present for the life you want to live. Give your full attention to the present moment or task at hand, rather than always thinking about what's next. Whether it's washing dishes or listening to a child's story, let your attention be fully there. We will return to this technique later when we discuss compartmentalizing.

A simple way is a great way to live your life. It is free of all the unnecessary things that the system wants us to buy, so there is only space for the absolute necessities. I don't know about you all, but this is my way to live my life. I hope you will one day find your way!

First Taste of Academic Pressure

My daily routine consisted of a lot of time in traffic. There was no socializing, no hanging out with friends after school. It was straight home. Dad would be back from work between 5 p.m. and 6 p.m. Dad and Mum would sit and talk about their day. We would have an Indian snack before dinner, around 6 p.m. Then it was dinner—also often Indian cuisine—at around 7:30 p.m., with me going to bed by 8:30 p.m. That was my typical day.

Weekends weren't all that different. It was study, study, study then as well. To be honest, our Nigerian lifestyle was as boring as it gets, as routine as it gets. Dad started building a bit of a social network with the Indian community. There was the odd weekend where we'd all go to the beach, or we'd have some sort of a social activity.

I was mostly very introverted and cheeky, and this had the effect of drawing a crowd. Everyone seemed to like me. All the elders, all the youngsters, they would gather around me. I didn't want to be a leader, mind you; I didn't want any power, but I had a certain cheekiness that I guess people found charming.

Other than these social interactions, weekdays were strictly about going to school, coming home, studying, and sleeping; while weekends were about the necessary chores, plus studying, and that was about it. It sounds a little dull, and I guess it was, but we needed that routine because, as I've mentioned, Lagos could be dangerous.

Around that time, military rule was being enforced throughout Nigeria. It was a time of serious geopolitical and economic tension. We would pretty much try to stay in our house whenever possible. Those forces, that tension, sometimes came into the house, sometimes broke into our seemingly safe little bubble.

The second serious incident that happened to my family occurred when we were coming back from the airport one night, a few years after the first. We had just returned from a trip to Europe. It was midnight, and we were travelling along a section of highway that connected the city to the airport, the road being lined by dense thickets of trees on either side. We must have slowed for one reason or another, and a bunch of guys, gang members most likely, jumped out in front of the car. Like before when our house was broken into, they saw me as an easy target and my parents' weak point. They pulled me out of the car, held a gun to my head, beat the crap out of the driver, and then took my parents' US dollars plus all their documents and gold. It was quite the "welcome back to reality" for us.

Once again, though, I felt only a sense of calm, believe it or not. Of course, I was scared. But it wasn't shocking. I thought to myself, "I've been through this once, how bad could it be?" So it was probably a little naïve of me to think that nothing serious could happen. But also, the naivety got me through it. I wasn't traumatized by it.

My parents on the other hand were traumatized, and right after that incident we went to a compound. We employed security guards with machine guns. We brought in huge dogs in cages.

But even then, there was another incident. This time they just slammed right through the gate. I don't know how they did it. They beat up the guards. I think they were sleeping so they didn't have time to react quickly. They tied them up and gagged them. Once again, they came into our house, and it was exactly the same as the first incident. They held me hostage and forced my parents to hand over cash and gold.

These were the three episodes that marked my time in Lagos, though for my father there would be a fourth. This was many years later, when he returned to Nigeria to run another business (even though he was supposed to be retired). He'd rented the same house we'd originally moved into all those years before, the one with the trees outside where the first break-in took place. I think he had a bit of a sentimental attachment to it. He had a colleague who reported to him, an Indian guy. They even had a security guard. Nevertheless, a band of burglars burst in in broad daylight, assaulted the security guard, gagged him, bound him, and came into the house. My dad was upstairs sleeping. They went up, dragged him out of bed, told him to get on his knees, put his arms behind his head, beat up his colleague who was around 40 years old. They stole all sorts of things but luckily didn't touch my dad, because of his age no doubt.

That's the weird thing about Nigerians; they have an interesting conscience, a complex view of the world, complex sense of right and wrong. They are some of the happiest people in the world; you see a certain good in them that you don't see in many developed countries. I started to see it as I was growing up with the drivers and the maids, and some of the Nigerian staff in my dad's company. They might have been broke, but they will bend over backwards to look after you. That's the sort of spirit that I saw in the Nigerian people. If you ask me, I would always say I'm a Nigerian at heart. I have Indian blood and a Nigerian heart!

Given the turmoil that raged in Lagos at the time, I was very happy to get to go to school. It was sort of a world unto itself. I loved going to school, even if the journey to school could be treacherous, because I knew that I would be seeing people, seeing friends, seeing my teachers. And from a very young age I found I was an adept manipulator. Or rather, I could get teachers on my side; I was sensitive to what they needed, or what they liked to see and hear, and I would oblige them. But rather than the manipulation being a negative thing, I think I was just ensuring I stayed out of trouble, that school would remain a more or less safe, even happy, environment without too many issues.

Having said that, I knew what I was doing. I wouldn't call it manipulation as such, but I knew that my grades hinged on what my teachers thought of me. Likewise, I knew that my social life hinged on my friendships, and so I did my best to give people what they liked, what they needed. I was always friendly and smiled a lot. I mean a *lot*. I love to smile. I was told as a kid that I smiled too much, and that I was too happy. But I would use that, in a way. Not that the teachers would automatically give me good grades, but from the outset I knew that getting good grades was more about fostering good relationships, which played right into the extroverted side of my personality.

One of the things that I do remember as a child was the academic pressure that I felt from my parents and from the community, because the Indian community is very competitive when it comes to grades. I never liked studying. Even today, I don't read too much. These days, I just observe and learn that way. When I was younger, I couldn't sit and read a book. I just couldn't be bothered. I didn't like it. I didn't like studying, didn't like sitting behind a desk. I had to learn Hindi, which was my national language, and I even hated learning that!

My saving grace was that I had a very good memory. I could memorize paragraphs and chapters of books and regurgitate them in the exams. But in general, I was a very poor student. If there were, say, 20 students in my class, I was often ranked right around the middle somewhere, dead centre, not terrific, not terrible. But my parents would want me to be in the top three. Which meant that I was invariably very scared to bring my report cards home!

The only exception was third grade. This was the only time I did well and placed in the top three. I remember proudly coming home; my dad was home for lunch because they'd already somehow heard the good news. I came home, I showed them my report card and I said, "I got in the top three." And they gave me a camera as a reward, as a gift. It was super old-fashioned, practically an antique. Still, I'd made them proud. Unfortunately, it was to be only a flash in the academic pan during my time in Nigeria. Things would get much better when I moved to America, but that was still a while off.

To be honest, doing poorly at school not only disappointed my parents, but actively incited their wrath, much to the agony of my backside!

Mum especially; she'd take a belt and chase me around the couch, threatening to teach me a lesson I clearly wasn't learning at school. In contrast, Dad had the cold stare but the warm heart. He'd tell me, "It's okay. Next time you'll be better." He was right, but that was a way in the future.

I think my parents worried about what sort of kid they had on their hands! They thought I was a bit weird, I'm sure. I just didn't seem to have the skills that were desirable within Indian culture. The idea was to be good academically, to excel at mathematics, to get straight A's. That's what makes Indian parents proud. But that wasn't my skill. I was, and remain, a people person. I could draw people in. My skills were more around making people happy, bringing people together, getting people on my side, which often meant that it cut both ways, it was good for them, and good for me as well. Which is to say that my skills were social as opposed to academic. I observed; that's what I was good at.

Caption: Contestant in a fancy dress competition when I was 7 years old; at a young age, may parents tried to bring me out of my shell and make me participate in extra-curricular activities

I used to observe the most athletic kids and ask myself what they did, how they behaved, how they drew a crowd. I would watch teachers and how they interacted with students. What made a teacher appreciate a student? Those were the things that I was more interested in. And those are the things that have stuck. It's common knowledge that whatever you learn in the first five or so years of your life is going to stick with you. That's what stuck with me. It has served me well in my life.

But in terms of grades it didn't serve me at all. I'd go back to India for an annual holiday, and my grandpa and grandma would say, "How are your grades?" And I'd say, "Ah, right yeah. Actually not the best." And, of course, my cousins were all doing amazingly, bringing home excellent grades. I was probably the worst performing kid in my entire family. But I didn't realize that I was probably one of the more popular people at our family gatherings, because I had a way with people.

Still, the comparisons were sometimes difficult for me. People would say, "Oh, such-and-such came number one in his class." Instantly, I knew where I stood, which often made me feel belittled or not up to scratch. It was around the subject of academic performance that I began to feel competitive—not that I worked harder, but rather I stood to turn into a sore loser. I began to carry something of a chip on my shoulder about it. This was something I would carry into my tennis down the track. Living your life in comparison to others is a recipe for unhappiness, and I certainly started to feel unhappy with my life in terms of my academic performance.

It was this period that instilled in me a need to prove myself, a need to get the best grade, a need to be number one. At that time, I wasn't good with pressure (well, not many people are under 10 years old!). I didn't know how to deal with it. I'd never really faced a situation in which I needed to perform under pressure. My upbringing was comfortable; in some ways it was perfect. I'd never faced stressful situations. These academic comparisons came with something called pressure, and because of my nature, and because of my upbringing, I wasn't sure how to deal with it.

To be honest, my poor performance at school, in academic terms, made me feel like I was a bit of a failure. So much so that I would, eventually, when I was about 10 years old, go to the extreme of doctoring my grades just so it would appear I was doing much better than I was. Safe to say, I was very aware of what others thought of me and, consequently, I was in a bind: I didn't value education, I wasn't very interested in it, and yet I wanted it to *appear* that I was interested, invested and proficient in it. I was more preoccupied with how things seemed than how they were. A recipe for unhappiness.

On returning to India each year, the comparisons always got worse. In fact, that's where they were made. Back in Nigeria, it was just Mum, Dad and I, so while I had my mother chasing me around the living room threatening to teach me lessons, it wasn't until the wider family got wind of my grades that the pressure started to mount. Luckily, my father worked for a company that had its head offices in London, and so he was exposed to a more European outlook. This proved to be something of a release valve for the pressure that was building up. If it wasn't for his trips to London, and our subsequent family trips all over Europe, I don't think my parents would have encouraged me to take up tennis the way they did. That was certainly not something traditional Indian parents would encourage.

Home Life

It's important to realize that my parents had an arranged marriage. They didn't really know each other beforehand. By now, they have been married for a very long time, but they had me very quickly, within a year of getting married. Which means that they had to get to know each other while I was growing up. That caused a fair bit of turbulence, tension, and verbal duels. My mother's a Leo and my father's a Scorpio, so things could get pretty volatile.

I learned a lot from what I observed in our home. (Now, my wife is a Leo; she was born on the same date as my mother, 5th August. Believe it or not, all the trouble I saw at home has helped me to become a pretty good husband.) The conflict I witnessed as a kid drove me to be a bit more reclusive and insular. I was worried about upsetting anyone or adding to the conflict. I would try to be the peacemaker, even though I didn't really know what I was doing. At times, however, the conflict would be so intense that I would be a little bit scared. I was always worried that something would set them off.

That's not to say that they didn't love each other deeply. They did; they still do. But during the early years, things could be on a knife's edge. For example, whenever my dad came home from work, we would have coffee or tea and some snacks before dinner. When they spoke calmly and quietly to each other I would experience the best feeling; really, it would make my day. Because everything would be calm and I'd be filled with relief.

In a way, though, it was understandable. They were so different, and they never spent time with each other prior to getting married. And then they had a child, which added a lot of pressure. On top of that, they were in Nigeria and far from home and family. So they really had to learn about each other, they had to learn about themselves, they had to learn to adapt, they had to learn to take care of me. All of these things together made for a high-pressure environment.

But for me, the likelihood of a flare-up, the tension around not knowing when the bomb would go off, had a significant impact. It probably set me on a path to pleasing people; these days I'm an expert in finding ways for people to get along and resolving their conflicts. While difficult, observing those conflicts, together with the family-oriented academic pressure, taught me valuable lessons and shaped me into the person I am today. My father was very relaxed and my mother was very intense, and so this combination kept me on my toes but gave me a sort of quiet confidence that everything would be okay. And so now, in the corporate world, I spend my time putting out fires, keeping calm even when it looks like the plane is about to crash.

Mounting Pressure

As you might have realized by now, while I was at school in Nigeria my grades weren't the best. I was a bit aimless; I hadn't found that "thing" yet, or at least realized it. My parents were worried about me. They thought perhaps this place, this system in Nigeria, was not the right fit for me. Maybe, they thought, I should go back to my home country; perhaps if I was exposed to that culture on a bigger scale, it might change my outlook and academic performance.

The main problem was that I simply did not like studying. There was no stimulation. I had no interest in anything academically; mathematics, English, Hindi, social science, science—I just couldn't care less.

So my parents took a calculated risk. They bought a house in Chennai, and I moved there with my mother for grade six. My dad didn't come.

But right from the time I landed, I didn't feel at home. It just didn't feel right. It was just Mum and I, so I had no fatherly figure for that year.

I'd travel to school on a rickshaw. Not a motorized one either! One poor guy would cycle all the way with three kids on the back like a miniature school bus. I must admit, I did enjoy that part of the day. I had a social thing where myself and two kids from my class would travel on a rickshaw every day to school and back. That was probably the highlight of my day.

But the Indian education system was even worse for me because everyone there was brilliant. Everyone was just so smart. Even the worst students seemed 10 times smarter than I was. I just couldn't absorb information. It was a real struggle. I was beginning to feel unstable. Mum didn't have Dad, so she was struggling a bit as well. The whole home atmosphere was not conducive to a stable family setting, and then going to a school where I just didn't feel comfortable didn't make for a happy world for me.

I was also struggling to find where I fit in. All the kids would play cricket before and after class, and I sucked at it, to put it mildly. I tried once and got bowled on the first ball. No, cricket was not for me. So I sat on the sidelines and watched all these cricket players being adored by other kids. I felt that everyone else had their thing, the thing that they excelled at or were at least good at, which seemed to me to fall into one of two categories: you were either good at schoolwork or good a cricket. Some people were, of course, good at both. But where did that leave me? Where was my sweet spot? What was my place here?

Added to this identity crisis, my grades were slipping rapidly. If I was averaging B's and C's in Nigeria, I was averaging C's and D's in India. I was feeling the pressure, and there was only one way I could find to release it.

I started to fudge my grades. Whenever I got a report card to take home I would doctor the grade to improve my score before showing it to my mother. If it was a C, I would make it look like an A and hope beyond hope that she wouldn't notice.

Unfortunately for me, my handiwork was not so handy after all! She saw right through it. She looked at me and said, "Is this your grade?" Perhaps I'd used a different ink. That's how idiotic I was. She said again, "Are you sure this is your grade?" Of course I said, "Yes." Alas, pretty quickly my mother put two and two together and what she came up with was not what was on the report card! If I'd been whipped before, now came time for the doozy, and I was left in no doubt as to the moral repugnance of my actions. Needless to say, I wouldn't try that again.

But I still couldn't accept the fact that I was not performing well. What happened next was the final straw, and I think it's what prompted the India experiment to end and I was sent back to Nigeria. Now, I was all too clear on the fact that I shouldn't doctor my reports; so that was out. I could still feel the blows to my backside. I wasn't going to risk that again.

This time, I took another report card, and I'd done so badly across all the classes that it wouldn't have paid to doctor them all even if I had a mind to. That would've been far too obvious. The question was, how can I erase this disaster completely? If I can't change my grades, how can I work it so that Mum doesn't see them at all? So in my brilliance I took the report and hid it in a drawer next to my bed. If I didn't show her the grades, the problem would magically disappear!

My mother is very particular about how the house is kept, always has been. She cleans absolutely everything. Even though we had a maid, she'd still go around and tidy things up. Always cleaning, folding, packing things away. No stone left unturned.

So, inevitably, the very next day after I'd smuggled the contraband of my bad grades into the house, I came home from school and she was waiting for me. "So," she said, glowering down at me, "what's this?" I said (actually, I probably mumbled), "That's my report card. I think I failed this one class." I figured if I said I only failed one class she wouldn't bother actually reading the thing.

With one hand she twisted my ear, while with the other she dialled my father in Nigeria. "This is not working," she screamed into the phone to him. "And we're coming back!"

I can see why my parents thought I should try India, but to me it just never felt right. And I think we could all see, though I was reluctant or incapable at that young age to do anything about it, that I was heading down a worrying road. If things had continued like that, who knows where I'd have ended up. Without a word of sarcasm, it might have even been jail. Things were not looking good.

Learning Empathy (The Hard Way)

Back in Nigeria, however, a terrible event was waiting for me, one that would impact my life significantly. It was my twelfth birthday and we were driving through town on the way to buy some clothes as a gift. I was in the front passenger seat, my mother was behind me in the back, and our driver was taking us where we needed to go. I was feeling good, because not only was it my birthday, but I also didn't have any tennis lessons that day.

I remember we were driving across a bridge when our car started veering across the road into the oncoming traffic. I didn't know at the time but our driver had fallen asleep at the wheel. Approaching rapidly from the opposite direction was a minibus. Our driver failed to wake up in time and we went head-on into it, a collision that produced a huge impact. I still have a scar on the right side of my forehead from where I hit my head on the dash. There was glass everywhere and I was bleeding terribly. Behind me, Mum had slammed into my seat and was in a bad way. As for the driver, he was not dead, but not far from it. He was completely unconscious.

Somehow, amidst the chaos, Mum got out and came around to my door, forced it open and carried me, almost like a dead person, flat on her two outstretched arms. Standing on the bridge, which is over an ocean inlet, connecting two islands, she was waving for someone to stop. Eventually someone did, and we were rushed to hospital.

I must have passed out or fallen asleep, for the next thing I knew my dad was next to me. My mum was not there. The doctor was saying something I didn't understand. Again, I passed out. Next thing I remember, I was home.

Mum had severe injuries to her legs and head, but would be okay. I had lost a lot of blood and they'd had to spend a long time picking pieces of broken glass out of me. One, so they said, had barely missed a critical artery. If Mum hadn't managed to get that car to stop for us, it was unlikely I would have survived.

Needless to say, it was a significant shock to the system. I now wore a full body cast, head to toe. I looked like a mummy! Life was difficult, to say the least, but I found that now, at school, I was receiving the kind of attention I'd been looking for all these years. I admit, I probably milked my injuries for all they were worth. My teachers had set me up with a special seat on the side of the classroom, and I sat there with a melancholic look about me. I wasn't really sad, of course; I was playing a game to see if I could get out of assignments, which actually worked a few times.

Believe it or not, there was something of an uplift in my grades that year. Perhaps it was because I could do nothing but my studies. Or that the teachers took a sort of pity on me, I don't know. Yes, I enjoyed the attention and special treatment, but also I received a slew of kindness, compassion and empathy from people who normally wouldn't give me the time of day. I saw that as a beautiful trait, from teachers, family and family friends. My accident put me in the driver's seat, if you'll excuse the bad pun, when it came to vulnerability. I'd never really thought about being vulnerable before, and here I was being vulnerable and receiving all sorts of kindnesses. And while I'd started out milking my injuries for special treatment, I ended up being pretty humbled by the experience, and grateful for the care people took with me.

These days, when I see that someone is being vulnerable, even when they don't voice it, I am sensitive to it; I can see it and make them feel comfortable with me. I try to show them the kindness that was shown to me. Some might say that's a bit of a weakness, because it puts me in a position where I can be easily taken advantage of, but there is a vast difference between being gullible and being sensitive to vulnerability.

Curiously, the accident taught me to receive help from others, which meant bringing down some barriers I'd put up to protect myself in this time of feeling like I was a failure. When I saw that kindness coming towards me, I felt I could open up more, which in turn created a much better rapport, a much better relationship, much better dynamic with the people I saw daily. Teachers and friends started seeing another side to me, a side that they were more comfortable to connect with. This connection meant that they too could open up to me.

These days, people seem to find it easy to be open with me, and I don't need to be in a cast for that to happen. That accident helped lift a veil or open a door, and I think the way that I come across now, the way that I communicate and my manner, sets people at ease, and encourages them to be open, honest and transparent with me, and we connect almost instantly. The crash, although terrible at the time, was actually a blessing in terms of my emotional openness, which has gone on to help me connect with people and form relationships with them, both in my personal life and my professional life. This in turn has helped facilitate all sorts of endeavours and projects that, at the end of the day, bear more fruit as a result.

Learning to Swim

To this day, I have one phobia and one phobia only, and that is deep water. I can jump out of planes, I can go bungee jumping. I've done all sorts of stupid things in my life, but you will never find me swimming in deep water.

Caption: Doing the 134m Nevis Bungy in New Zealand

This all stems, I think, from when I was a kid, when my mother would bathe me. One day she put too much water over my face. It was a shock, and I felt, even though it was only for a moment, that I was suffocating. From that time on, I've had trouble swimming. I mean, I can swim, but I just can't get the swimming and breathing rhythm going. It scares the hell out of me! We learned this the hard way when my parents thought

I should go for swimming lessons. As soon as the instructor tried to teach me how to breathe while swimming, I panicked. I just couldn't do it. After three lessons, we put an end to that idea.

To this day, I go to the beach for a barbecue and to look at the stars. I don't go to the beach to swim or surf or anything like that. Which annoys my wife, I think, because she's an avid swimmer. I can't really swim with her, which is a shame. Also, living in Australia, everybody swims; swimming is ingrained in the culture, so being left sitting on the sand can be a bit of a drag.

The First Thing I Was Ever Good At

My involvement in tennis came out of my dad's love for the sport. He was a member of a club in Lagos, and he would play every Sunday morning. It would take over an hour to get there in the go-slow. But he was such an avid lover of tennis, it was apparently worth it. He would meet three of his friends at this club and take me along as ball-boy.

I saw this as a huge treat, to hang out with him and watch him play a very cool sport with three of his friends. I was about eight years old. I loved swooping in and picking up the balls. I felt very important hanging out with these four adult men, and for them to take a ball from me gave me a lot of happiness; it felt like they needed me. I always looked forward to those Sundays.

One particular Sunday, one of Dad's friends had injured his hamstring. So, to my astonishment, my dad said, "Okay, let's give the racquet to Kaushik and let him play." I hadn't had a single lesson. I'd never had a hit back and forth with friends. Nothing. I didn't even own a tennis racquet.

But I had watched, I had observed. And this is my strength. Observation. So I took the racquet on that auspicious Sunday, and when the first shot came to me I simply put the racquet behind the ball and it soared across the net and we won the point. I didn't realize that it was a big deal. I just thought that was what I was supposed to do, get the ball over the net. And so I did.

When we came home that day, my dad said to my mum, "This kid's all right at tennis. He has real potential. Why don't we invest in some lessons?" For the first time, I think they saw a glimmer of a direction for me, something that might carry me through and possibly lead to other things.

They got me this little purple tennis racquet, which I adored. I still have it in India. And so I started taking lessons. Initially it was once a week. We'd finish school and then my mum and I would go through the go-slow, a very arduous journey just to get to the tennis club. It was about three kilometres from home, but it would take an hour to get there because of the traffic. I enjoyed the lessons immensely. They made sense to me; I could see myself getting better, I could see the progression. Unlike a few other things I tried at the time—cricket, academia, I even took singing lessons—I felt like with tennis there was a future.

The lessons were once a week, and then it became twice a week, then three times a week. It was fun. The reason it was fun was that it was an hour in which I could escape into an athletic setting. The other beauty was my mum would give me a bottle of Coca-Cola during each session. She knew I loved Coca-Cola so much, and so she said, "Okay. Because it's so hot and humid, you can have a Coke or a Fanta between your breaks." She'd buy this huge 30-bottle crate of soft drink and keep it at home; I'd take one with me each time we left for the club. It was another incentive for me to keep playing tennis!

Caption: My first-ever tennis racket

Caption: Practising a serve with my first tennis coach in Nigeria

I was becoming quite good, I thought, because I was consistently hitting the ball over the net, which doesn't sound like much but when you're less than 10 years old, it's something. I remember my mum and the coach would chat, and the coach would say this word, tournament. I didn't know what that word meant. But it was one that would have a dramatic impact on my life.

Before I knew it, I was signed up for this thing called a tournament in Lagos in the under-10 category. I played, and to my surprise I won. But, to be honest, I could have won the tournament blindfolded. Now, I didn't think I was that good at all, but when I got on that court everything just happened so seamlessly. It felt like I didn't have to put in any effort at all. It just clicked. I didn't even know I'd won until they handed me this little trophy. But the best trophy wasn't the small plastic thing they awarded me at the court; rather, it was when we got home and I saw Dad's eyes beam with pride and excitement. I'd never seen him like that before in my life. It gave me more motivation to keep going and not give up.

I kept playing. Now, on weekends, my dad strategically made me one of his team of four. Somehow he got rid of the fourth person, or that person pulled out of the regular sessions. And so I became the fourth person in those Sunday tennis matches.

Funnily enough, I very quickly became bored with it because I was too good for them. It was just so boring! With all the training I was doing, all the hours I was putting in, I was leaving the adults behind. But, although it wasn't much competition, I still went. Sometimes I'd still play the role of ball boy. When my father got tired of being beaten, he brought that fourth member back!

Being an only child, it was up to me to keep myself occupied. And what I started doing was, because I couldn't go out and meet friends in the evening (too dangerous), I would play myself in tournaments. I'd hit the ball against a wall at home. Inside the house, mind you, not outside, which was undoubtedly the source of many headaches for my mum and dad.

But I would seriously play myself. I'd write down scores and I'd play like there was no tomorrow. I'd play until well into the night, just banging the ball against the wall until I won the tournament. I would be 64 different players and play my own little Wimbledon against myself. I did that every evening and loved it. It's probably something about me. I just like to pretend that I'm someone competing against myself.

Soon enough I was placed into more tournaments. I competed against the under-12s, even under-14s, which was way above my age group. Nevertheless, I'd win. In Nigeria, I would win those tournaments. So I was winning a lot and had a really good ranking.

Then came the turning point in my life. There was something called an inter-school competition in Nigeria. You had an American school, a British school, an Indian school, and of course the Nigerian school. Many different schools competed, each with its own cohort of ex-pat students and players.

At this point, in my school, I was a nobody. I was always behind the scenes. I had a few friends here and there, but I certainly wasn't the popular kid. I was not the centre of attention. There were kids who were amazing at basketball. They were all growing tall rapidly. I was not tall. I was short by comparison. These kids were all socially active, extroverted, popular, the whole bit. The girls swooned around them. I was starting to do well at tennis, but still didn't really have a place. That was all about to change.

For the first time, the principal of our school was putting together a tennis team to compete at the inter-school competition, which was like the schoolyard version of the Davis Cup. The principal came to me and said, "Kaushik, you're going to be one of the four." I felt a pressure fall on my shoulders because I thought, "I'm going to represent this school where I'm a nobody. If I fail, what's that going to do to my reputation?" I didn't say anything at the time. I just shrugged and agreed. I kept those sorts of things to myself, which was why my parents worried about me. They saw me internalizing a lot of things growing up. In any case, I tried to keep the pressure to myself. I was not sure how I was going to perform.

The day came, and we went to this big stadium. I'd never been in this sort of environment before. The stands, the courts, and also, something I hadn't experienced before, there was a crowd. And a big one at that! There was a massive crowd of Americans, Brits, Africans and Indians. Something about that crowd had an odd effect on me; I was all at once calm, excited and relaxed. You would normally expect a bit of nerves when you see an audience. But I liked it straight away. I soon found that I would thrive on it.

My first match was against an American. The match barely lasted half an hour. I won before I knew it. I didn't realize I was beating him until it was over. I only realized I'd performed well when I heard the great round of applause from the crowd. This was not just the Indian school, either; this was all four ethnicities. That's when it first hit me that it was something special. Maybe I had something that not many others have. It was something I could begin to have a bit of confidence in.

Then we played the doubles. I was paired with another Indian kid who was very popular at our school. Next to him I was practically invisible. But after the first serve, things just fell into place. We won the match, and afterwards he gave me a hug and said, "You're amazing!" I haven't forgotten that. It made me quite emotional at the time. It made me so happy to feel recognized by someone that I looked up to as a social champion in school. It was extraordinary to feel included.

Then came the final game of the day. It was between me and another kid from our school. I managed to beat him, and then next day it was someone from another school, and after that was the finals. The pattern that I'd started with continued all the way through that tournament, which our school would go on to win.

Just how much of an impact I had made, came to me the day after the final when we were back at school. Every morning we had an assembly where we stood in line, sang the national anthem, and the principal said a message. She had me stand next to her, which was a treat, usually. She had a raised platform and made me stand on it because I was so short, so I could be just a bit taller than her and everyone in that assembly could see me. As part of her message that day, she said, "We are the champions. This is Kaushik. Give him a round of applause." And the whole school erupted into cheers.

I still cherish the memories of that tournament and that assembly. I'll cherish it forever because it was the first time I'd felt special. It gave me tremendous confidence. It made me think that I'm a bit different to others. Academically speaking, everyone was a genius at that school. Yes, I'd won a dress-up competition (don't ask), and I'd won a singing competition, so I was seen as a bit weird; but with the tennis stuff, that was something that everyone recognized and responded to collectively. At the same time, however, I was learning to appreciate the benefits of learning to be skilled in many areas, and how enriching that is.

Lesson 2: You Can Be a Master of Many Things

Yes, one day you will be dead. But it takes about seven years to master something. If you live to be 88, after age 11, you have 11 opportunities to be great at something. Most people let themselves die and cling onto that one life. But you can spend a life writing poem, another life building things, and another life looking for facts. You have many lives. Live them.

In my life, I've turned my hand to many things and found satisfaction in nearly all of them. From playing tennis, to coaching, to teaching and lecturing at a university level, to public speaking, to travel and my work in the corporate world; I've learned to do many, many things. And I've been successful at them; not by any generalized definition of the term "successful", but by my own standards. Ask yourself what success means to you. It probably won't mean wealth and fame; with any luck it'll be something deeper than those. Only you can determine what being successful means. And once you've defined that, you can decide how you want and need to spend your time.

I believe that the most valuable personality is someone who knows something about everything and everything about something. So it's valuable to have a little knowledge of math, physics, chemistry, biology, geography, history, sociology, economics, and so forth. Having a complete gap in any of those subjects is a bad thing. But clearly you can't learn deeply about such a wide spread of things.

Knowing a lot about a relatively small slice of that is also important— especially if you'd like a decent job that pays good money. Most really good jobs require a greater depth of knowledge about the specific field that the job relates to.

Being interested in "too many things" isn't a problem—you can gradually increase your depth of knowledge in those things at whatever rate life allows. But finding just one or perhaps two of those things to become a "deep" expert in is something you should work hard to do.

Are there any of those things that you have slightly more interest in than the others? Find that one thing and do a deep dive into the subject. Continually push at the bits you don't (yet) fully understand.

Back before Wikipedia had an article about almost everything, I'd often pick something that hadn't been written about and try to learn enough to write a decent article about it. That was an incredibly useful trick to get my mind to focus on one small area and dive deeper and deeper into it. Tracking down all of the small leads is as much of a compelling thing as reading widely but shallowly. Recently, I've been doing the reverse: which is to answer lots of questions on LinkedIn, which requires a very broad (but relatively shallow) knowledge of a lot of things. Alternating between these two modes of thinking has proven incredibly stimulating. I think you just need to take a swing at the narrow-but-deep part. If you're at all smart, you'll enjoy the change —and it'll certainly benefit your life to be a deep expert in a few things.

But it's not one-or-the-other. You can be a "Jack of all trades and master of one or two."

Tennis Becomes My Life

My success on the court spurred me on to go further with tennis. To practice harder. To get better and better. I entered more tournaments. And I started winning. I wanted to win. I loved to feel good about winning. I didn't win everything that I played, but I started winning a lot of tournaments, and people at school just saw me differently, started holding me in higher regard, recognizing me in the halls.

It wasn't so much that I was receiving special treatment from the teachers. Rather, it was my classmates and other students who seemed to take the most notice. But even the principal would look at me differently. Because, in an Indian environment, you're judged on the basis of your grades and the principal will usually give their attention to the highest-performing students. That's usually how the politics work; it's always about grades. But here was an athlete, or an aspiring athlete, who had become close to the key stakeholders at a very senior level. I was starting to recognize my own value, and to make it work for me in my own way.

After a few years, I was ranked number one in Nigeria, and I was starting to catch the eyes of some influential people. At the time, my dad's boss was one of the wealthiest men in the UK (in part, thanks to my dad). Whenever he came to Nigeria, he spent time with my father who told him about my tennis. He was one of the key people who pushed my dad to encourage my tennis game. In fact, I think part of the reason my dad was so passionate about pushing me was his boss; or, at least, his boss opened a door to his thinking that I could make a go of it.

I had reached the ranking of number one by the age of 12. It was at this point that a tennis school in Texas, as part of their recruitment drive, had found out about me. By that time my name was becoming quite well-known. It was in newspapers, popping up here and there in the media. It's important to remember that, in Nigeria, there weren't many non-Nigerian athletes in the top echelon. And now here I was, a kid from India. I looked different in the photos. I sounded different in interviews. There were things being written up about my forehand and about my quick acceleration to becoming number one.

One day my parents received a letter asking them if I would like to go to a tennis academy run by a famous Australian tennis player in Texas. On a full scholarship, no less. I think they were eager to have a famous athlete come out of their school; at that time, it was pretty much just one other tennis school in Florida pumping out a whole range of big names. But this academy only had one, a lesser-known doubles tennis player, who was number one.

I don't think my parents knew quite what to do. Apparently they consulted my father's boss, who was Indian but based in the UK. He had a worldlier outlook, so they asked him what he thought about it all. "Bloody take it!" was his advice.

Deep down, though, my parents were worried about letting go of me. Of course they were. I'm also sure there were other things concerning them; with my blended personality and the bumpy ride we'd had till then, I'm sure they were forecasting issues that might come up.

It was around this time that my dad's father passed away. I hadn't really encountered a family death until then. I remember coming home from school and receiving the news. We'd been moving houses every three years or so, trying to find a safer environment within Lagos; but this new place, it was one of my favourite houses that I ever lived in. I came back from school, my snack was on the table, and I found my dad in tears. I'd never seen that before. It's quite upsetting for a young son to see his father break down like that. It was my mum who told me. Dad was too upset. So I went to him, fell on his lap and started crying. He had to go to India for the funeral, and consequently America was temporarily put on hold.

But soon enough he was back and we were able to focus on our lives again. I still remember sitting together in the living room and my parents explaining to me what the opportunity meant. For example, I didn't know that I would be going alone, living away from them. I didn't know what it would feel like to leave my parents. I didn't know what America was. We had taken trips to Europe, but I was just a kid looking at the Eiffel Tower, not really ensconced in the culture.

My dad laid it out for me in no uncertain terms: It was a great opportunity.

I looked at my mum. It was now her turn to be in tears. I think we all knew what the outcome was going to be. I was going. It *was* a great opportunity, one that could make or break me. I placed myself in the hands of fate—something I would do over and again in my life—and so began the next chapter of my life. Little did I know how turbulent the years ahead of me would be, even leaving aside the near plane crash that could have extinguished my dream before it had begun. Nevertheless, I was learning that winging it comes hand-in-hand with embracing what I like to call Good Scary!

Lesson 3: Good Scary

Getting out of your comfort zone is, by definition, uncomfortable. It's easier to say "no" to opportunities that feel scary. But many of the best decisions I have made felt scary at first. When we talk about saying no to things, it is important to note the *reason* for saying it. We're not saying no because the thing is scary or uncomfortable. We say no in cases where saying yes does not align with our goals and ambitions for our lives. We do have a great self-preservation system embedded in our DNA, which is always on the lookout for scary situations. It's trying its best to protect us. But it doesn't know the difference between "good scary" and "bad scary". All it knows is scary! Good scary is venturing out of your comfort zone to realize a goal and better your life. And it's in these situations that we need to override our body's tendency to play it safe. Yes, change is scary, but that's no reason to say no to it!

Part Two

America

Leaving Childhood Behind

Eventually, following our detour to Shreveport, Louisiana and the incident that nearly dashed all our plans, we made it to the tennis academy in Texas. The first three days were spent in orientation. We met the academy's administrator who gave us the rundown on what would become my daily schedule for the next few years: waking up, gym, schooling, and of course tennis.

I wasn't really paying attention. It was all so new and so different; I didn't know which way to look. The place was like Mars to me. I hadn't seen such a pristine environment before, and I was also slowly starting to comprehend the reality that lay before me. Which is to say, the idea of being away from my parents was slowly starting to sink in.

We visited the tennis courts. I had a hit with some of the local players, to give the coaches an idea of my skills. Everyone got along. My parents were happy with it. I think, despite their obvious anguish of having to let me live in a different country, they were happy.

But I wasn't feeling it. Something about the academy didn't sit well with me; I didn't feel comfortable. It wasn't so much the alien environment. Rather, the whole place resembled a sort of army barracks. Everything was very regimented, and the tight schedules we were going to be on seemed like boot camp. This was an environment I definitely wasn't used to. Things just weren't like that where I'd come from.

Following that initial orientation, we flew back to Nigeria. My parents had to finalize things with the academy, signing my life away in terms of enrolments, living arrangements, even my diet. Incidentally, I never did meet the founder of the academy, despite it being his academy. He was never there.

Back in Nigeria in June, reality sunk in. We now had a date: August 1997. That's when my life would change for good. Not via some freak accident, of which I'd been involved in a few to date, but because of a choice I'd made—or rather, a choice my parents had made and I'd gone along with. Soon I'd be leaving my childhood behind, in more ways than I knew in June of 1997.

Now, a confession. Throughout my entire childhood up until that point in my life, I had a bedwetting problem. It was just a thing that I did. It happened every night, without fail. It is important to note that while I was often calm and focused during a crisis, the flipside was that, in the absence of crisis, in everyday life, I was something of a nervous child. Maybe it was a response to my parents' volatile relationship; having to navigate a household constantly on edge. Maybe it was being out of my comfort zone having moved to a new country. Whatever it was, my nervousness often came out, if you'll excuse the pun, as bedwetting. It was part of our daily routine as a family. Every morning, my dad would be soaked and we'd have to change the sheets. It was a very uncomfortable thing, but I didn't realize it was uncomfortable and my parents didn't make a big deal of it. Which was a blessing, really, because if they had, it would have been much worse.

The reason I share this with you is that, once that date in August was set, one of the things I was most concerned about was the fact that I was still wetting the bed. How would my life be in a foreign country, where I knew no one and was trying to make friends, living in a dormitory with at least one other boy, if I was wetting the bed every night? It filled me with horror. But seemingly there was nothing I could do about it!

August came and we had to leave. It was just my dad and I, as Mum was staying behind. I think it was a bit too much for her.

I remember saying goodbye to my mum. It was overwhelming for her, but it was still sinking in for me. I think I was still too worried and a bit bamboozled by the whole situation to be able to cope with the nuances of everyone's emotions at the time.

Still, like it or not, we were getting on that plane to Texas. My dad accompanied me and we'd spend three nights together before he went back to resume life and we'd all have to get used to our new normal.

To my horror and dismay, I was still wetting the bed. Even after we'd arrived, and my father and I were in the apartment we'd booked for those three days, there it was. What else did I expect? I had been doing it all my life; it was silly to think it would just vanish.

It came to our last morning together, the morning that would see him fly off and leave me here alone. Unbeknownst to me, he had arranged for one of the students, a New Zealander to come to the room and escort me to my new dormitory. I think he forecasted how I might be reacting to everything.

So I woke up that morning in a complete panic. My heart was going at 5,000 beats a minute. I checked the sheets. Maybe this time I hadn't, maybe just this once.

But no, I had done it. Once again, I'd wet the sheets. So I got up, got dressed. I didn't want to go. I refused. I was crying like there was no tomorrow. The New Zealander arrived, ringing the bell from the door below. The time had come. I had to go. But I didn't want to go. I felt that I couldn't go. My father buzzed him in, and while he was making his way up to our room, my father sat down and looked me right in the eye.

He said to me, "You are doing this for the right reasons. You'll always get two chances a year to come and see us, during Christmas and during your summer break. It's not like this is goodbye forever. This is a golden opportunity for you to become a successful tennis player."

It was a wretched day. My dad tells me that he watched me walk away with the New Zealander, my little, short steps, not wanting to go. Apparently, I kept looking back crying. But then we made a turn, and that was it. That was the last moment of my childhood. That was when I moved from being a child to being an adult. For me, that remains a very important moment.

For the first time in my life, I had a single bed to myself. I'd never even slept in a single bed before; it had always been Mum, Dad and I in the family bed. Now, here I was on the other side of the planet, alone on a small bed. That first night I just lay in that bed, staring at the ceiling, trying to comprehend what had just happened.

I don't know if I had some harsh words with myself, if I said, "It's time to grow up." I still don't know exactly what happened. But that night in August of 1997 was the start of the next phase of my life, for that night in that single bed was the first night in my entire life that I didn't wet the bed.

Healthy Body, Healthy Mind

For the next four years, this was my routine: We'd wake at 5 a.m. and get straight into training, running, and aerobic exercises. Then we'd come back, have breakfast in the cafeteria, which was followed by room-cleaning then off to school. At lunchtime we'd return to our dorms, get changed into our tennis clothes, and it was into a classroom for about half an hour to talk about aspects of tennis with our coaches. After that, from 2 p.m.-6 p.m. we were on the court, training, practicing, playing. From 6-6:30 p.m., it was yet more exercise, running usually. This was tough, after a day of physical activity to get hit with more running drills. To be fair, though, we were very fit! After that it was home for showers, 6:45 dinner, study from 7:30-8:30 p.m., followed by an hour of free time before lights out at 9:30 p.m. That was my routine, five days per week, with a slightly longer free-time period on Friday evenings.

That didn't mean we got off lightly on the weekends; we still trained between 9 a.m.-12 p.m., then the afternoons were usually filled with planned excursions to the mall or an ice-skating rink. To be honest, other than the excitement of playing tennis, life was fairly dull.

Bullying and Isolation

It was pretty clear from the get-go that I stood out. I'm Indian, of course, so I automatically stood out in a predominantly Caucasian student cohort. But there were other things that set me apart. To be honest, my dressing style was pretty terrible, from a Western perspective. It was quite colourful, like all the Bollywood actors. I looked like a rainbow! I also, as I'd always done and as my mother had done for me, put coconut oil in my hair. I put a bit of the holy ash on my forehead. And my accent also made me stand out. I pronounced things differently like, "we" instead of "V", which was to be something in the very near future that would attract a lot of unwanted attention. In the end, though, I was a typical Indian kid going to a school that was very Western, in Texas.

I was completely unaware of people judging me. In my mind, I was always the observer. I always looked at what others did and thought about what others did. I'd always flown under the radar at school (until I started becoming successful at tennis, but then the attention was always favourable). In America, I had no idea that people were looking at me and making judgements. I was just in my own little bubble.

At school some of the lecturers couldn't pronounce my name. I remember, in my first science class, the teacher kept trying to get his tongue around the name; he kept saying, "Kursch, Kash, Kursch," (which only gave others more ammunition to fire at me). Even when I told him how to pronounce it, he just couldn't seem to grasp it. It made me feel quite scared. I was the only brown person in that room. (To be honest, this still happens in the corporate world from time to time!)

There were a few people with black skin at the academy, and only a few, but I was the only brown-skinned kid there. The rest were just all white. Oddly enough, the way that I saw things coming from Nigeria, black and white was the same thing. They were the majority. Also, I didn't know that there was a divide between black and white in America. I saw them as one big majority. Which left me, the brown-skinned kid.

I was very much a lone wolf. When I went to the lunch cafeteria, I'd get my food and take it to a table with something like 20 unoccupied seats. Still, nobody would sit with me. Black people and white people were hanging out together, more or less, but brown was left alone.

Speaking of eating. Before my dad left me, he said, "Kaushik, you're a Hindu. You've been a vegetarian all along, but for tennis you've got to eat meat because you need to build muscle. So if you eat meat, it's okay. Don't worry about it."

He was very cool that way. He was not all that religious. So I actually started eating chicken, beef, meat for the first time in my life! I loved it. Absolutely loved it. I tasted something that I wish I'd been tasting for a long time. From my first day, my intake of vegetables went down and the meat went way up. It was so delicious. I didn't know what I'd been missing! I was eating this marvellous food, but I was eating it alone.

And of course, pretty quickly there was the issue of girls. Let's call her Kristen, and she was a part of the tennis academy. I thought she was the cutest girl there. What was even more miraculous, she was four years older than me. Of course, I'd noticed her, but never even considered approaching her. That would have been instant death! One day, however, I found out from someone else that she thought I was cute too. This was another situation where I couldn't tell which way was up. It didn't quite compute. All of a sudden I'd landed splat in the middle of a foreign country all over again! She thought that I was cute? But I was simply too shy, and so I did nothing. Even when, eventually, she did approach me a few times to say nice things, I would always remain evasive and nervous. For some reason, this sort of thing happened quite often, but I was too young to realize that I should nurture those relationships.

I remember there was a fire alarm at school. We were all standing outside, and one girl came up to me and said, "My friend, she's over there in the pink top. She wants to get your number to take you out."

Again, I was dumbstruck. I think I blurted out something like, "No, no. I can't do it!"

My tennis buddies were standing next to me. Of course, they were saying, "You're such a loser, Kaushik. What's *wrong* with you?" I didn't understand anything about girls or dating. Rather than act and find out, I hid away in my shyness. So that was another angle of attack that opened up for those with a mind to attack me. Combined with the way I dressed, my accent, my skin colour, and the way I smelled–it was all a rich blend to be classed as an outcast.

Meanwhile, tennis was going well. In those first few months I was winning a lot. We played tournaments within the academy, with matches twice a week. We were competing with each other, and if you won, you went up the ladder. There was a ladder for the 30 of us in my group, and I was climbing it nicely. I was beating some very promising players. The coaches loved me because I was the youngest and also promising. I even heard whispers about me becoming the next Sampras!

Little did I know that my reputation was about to be dealt yet another blow. Unbeknownst to me, my parents had organized my entire curriculum, all my classes, the subjects I would take, plus all my extracurricular activities. Which meant that they'd enrolled me in the school choir! Of course, I'd done a bit of singing in the years before, but I genuinely thought we'd left that all behind us by now. Alas, that was not to be.

There was no two ways about it: I was in a choir. To be fair, it a nice group, but my voice was like a girl's. I could hit the high notes usually reserved for the girls. My singing teacher loved me, and encouraged me to be in as many concerts as my schedule would allow. According to her, I had a very promising voice. But I was more interested in being Pete Sampras, rather than Justin Bieber.

Maybe it was my background, but I thought it was more of a feminine thing to sing. To be honest, I was embarrassed about it. After the first year of high school, I quit, much to my parents' annoyance. That was the last time that I sang. I just couldn't keep it up. To my surprise, I'd started making decisions for myself at that time without realizing it.

On the other hand, the tennis was going swimmingly. I was certainly in the top half of my group, which, when you did the math, the top quarter were going to go on and have professional tennis careers and rank in the top 100 in world tennis. So things were on the up.

I was playing very well but, unfortunately my social life started to take a nosedive. One evening, several months into that first year at the academy, I was lying in the common room watching television, just chilling out, when my roommate's five friends came in and started asking me questions: "Why do you dress the way you do? Have you heard of a brand called Tommy Hilfiger? Have you heard of GAP?" They were laughing at me. Of course, I had no idea who or what they were talking about.

They made fun of everything that I represented, but I didn't realize it was racism, I didn't know it was bullying. In fact, I just thought, "Oh, okay. They just think differently to me, and that's okay." I'd always been taught to just accept things, and I accepted their poor behaviour without questioning or standing up for myself.

Then the next day they came back. I think they saw an opportunity in my vulnerability.

This was when the real trouble began; the physical as well as the emotional bullying. The next day, they came into the common room with an even bolder energy, this time there was an aggressive tone in their voices. They started slapping me on the head, saying things like, "You're Indian. You're from a shitty country. Your accent is like Apu from Simpsons. What do you think you're doing here trying to become a tennis player?!"

I tried to ignore and accept it all, just as I had always done.

I just kept playing tennis and kept doing my thing. During the one-hour break time each evening, I continued to visit the common area, but was careful not to just lie around. I started playing table tennis. That was my outlet. I became very good at it, if I do say so myself. I taught myself to play it, and I had a lot of time in which to practice. It was what I did to cope with the bullying; I immersed myself in learning table tennis every night. I practiced and practiced and practiced, just as I was doing with tennis during the day. In fact, it was probably very good for my tennis game. It is something I keep up even to this day. But back then, each night I would beat the living crap out of that ping pong ball as a way to vent my feelings. I came to own that table.

Meanwhile, I had to continue focussing on tennis. That's what I was there for. That's why I had that scholarship, and why both me and my parents were sacrificing a lot.

I had a rhythm, I had a pattern. I was able to block out a lot of the negative energy, even at the cafeteria. Eventually I fell in with a very quirky group of kids, a very eccentric sort of group. There were five of us around that table, which was so nice, to have some friends outside of the tennis academy, just regular school friends. That was beautiful.

But then those one-hour breaks became increasingly turbulent. That group of boys would come into the room and corner me on my single bed. I remember vividly. They would start with the verbal stuff, and then they would beat me. Initially it was just one person punching my chest, my legs, my back. Soon, though, the others joined in, two guys, three guys. Even my roommate would punch me. The most wretched thing was then I'd have to sleep with him in the same room.

In a strange way, I thought I deserved it. I didn't feel that I was being bullied as such. I felt that I brought it on myself for being different, for not being cool, because I wasn't like them.

Because they were part of the academy, they would travel in the bus with me when we'd play tournaments. Sometimes just seeing them watching me while I was on court could ruin a match for me.

Still, I was performing well at those tournaments, despite it all. I was winning. My tennis star was still rising, despite me getting (physically) beaten. But, I think, somewhere inside me, somewhere deep down, my passion for the sport was reducing, without me even realizing it.

But then it would be back to campus and the beatings would continue. On one hand, I was winning tournaments, collecting all these trophies. I was feeling pretty good about that; somehow I was able to shut off the other side of my life and feel good about the progress I was making in the world of sport.

But every weekend I would have a call with my parents on a payphone. They called from a public telephone and I would talk to them for about 30 minutes. It was very expensive to call from Nigeria at that time. Luckily, my dad's company paid for everything because he was an ex-pat. During these calls I'd delight in telling them everything that was happening with my tennis, how well it was going. And they seemed very happy about it all. I held back on the other things, the negative things. I stuck to the good news. That's partly just the way I am; I tend to focus on the positives and shut out the negatives. If I gave the bullying more airtime while I was talking to my parents, not only would it have worried them, it would invade a relationship that served as a sort of escape for me. While talking to my parents, I could forget about academy life. I didn't want to drag the stresses of my everyday life into my time with my parents.

Also, lo and behold, I was doing well in school! For the first time in my life I was getting good grades. The Western education system is so different to that in the East. Honestly, it was so much easier for me in America in that respect. Mathematics, calculus, whatever it was, I breezed through it. My GPA shot up to 3.9, which meant I was getting mostly A's and B's. I was so happy that I could finally tell my parents, "I was top of the class in year nine, or top in year 10. And I won all these tournaments."

As far as they were concerned, I was doing very well, having a good time, meeting people, getting good grades and winning at tennis. They had no idea what else was going on. How could they?

Then, one day, that group of guys came in to my dorm room and yet again laid into me. It was a particularly bad one; I received a severe beating. It was a Sunday, and Sunday was also the day that I spoke to my parents. So after this beating, I had to go and speak to my mum and dad. They were going to call, and there was no way of getting a message to them saying not to call. It wasn't like I could sent a text message or anything. You made a time, and you stuck to it.

I ran to the payphone, battered and bruised. When I picked up the phone, my mum could hear something different in my voice. She said, "What's wrong?" I tried to brush it off. I told her nothing was wrong. She asked again and again, and I kept trying to put her off. Eventually she put her foot down, and I knew better than to argue. She said, "No, you need to tell me. I'm your mother!"

I tried to downplay it, saying something like, "Oh, I just had a small incident with some of my friends." (I called them my friends to take the edge off.) But she kept pressing me; maybe she sensed there was more to it. Which, of course, there was.

She said, "Okay. Tell me. I'm asking you for the last time." She was getting annoyed, and that always scared me. So I came clean and told her about the bullying, about the beating that had happened that morning. After a brief silence, she said, "I'm going to put your dad on the phone."

Then I had to repeat it to my father. But by then, the cat was out of the bag, so I just told him straight: "I've been getting the shit beat out of me for the last six months by six boys. That's how life's been."

For the next minute or so, there was nothing on the other end of the line. Complete radio silence. I think he was in some sort of anguish or pain. But for a full 60 seconds, neither of us said anything. I had to ask if he was still there. Now his voice was a little shaky. But also there was a darkness to it. I could sense another side of Dad coming out, a side I had seen before but one that I didn't know I would inherit until years later.

Then he said, "Okay. Today's Sunday. What I want you to do is keep your mouth shut. Tonight you will eat your food and go to sleep." And so that's what I did.

The next day, I had arrived back at the academy after school. I'd gotten out of the van, and one of the coaches was waiting. He gently took me aside from everyone else. He said, "Let's go for a walk. Let's have a chat." He didn't say that he knew anything, and I just thought he was checking in on me or something, as though this was something routine he did with everyone. So I kept out all the negative stuff, and just told him what a great time I was having. What I didn't know was that my father had been on the phone to them and had somehow struck the fear of God into the entire establishment. I still don't quite know how he did it.

It was time for our afternoon briefing, which we had every day before hitting the courts. But I was still talking with one of our coaches. I told him I was worried I would miss the briefing. But he assured me that it was fine and that we should just hang back a bit.

Eventually though, we went into that briefing room together. We were about 10 minutes late. All the students were gathered there. Everyone's face was frozen, including the six bullies but everyone else as well. It was like they were in shock. As I came in, all necks turned towards me. Silence.

I was late, and I had indeed missed the briefing. But it was one that I didn't need to hear. Because, apparently, it had gone something like: "If anyone lays a finger on Kaushik again, you will be expelled immediately." That's basically the message that was given in that briefing, nothing else.

After everyone had left for the courts, the coaches once again held me back and told me, "We've had a word with your parents and nothing like this will happen again."

For a moment, it was welcome relief. But what I didn't know was that this was only going to make things a whole lot worse. Things were about to spiral out of control. Tennis and that place was never the same after that day. That Monday marked a turning-point where my love for tennis and my desire to be in Texas, started to leave me.

The Pressure Gets the Better of Me

So began the downward spiral. I'm not sure if the bullying was fully to blame for what came next, but it certainly was a catalyst. If I was isolated before, now it became even more pronounced. The physical abuse stopped, but now the emotional bullying kicked off. And it wasn't just the six boys from before; they had friends who had friends, and the circle of people out to make my life miserable seemed to widen exponentially overnight.

I requested a change of room; I didn't want to live with that guy anymore. I was moved to a room with an excellent Chinese tennis player. But he could barely speak any English, so there wasn't a great opportunity to bond.

But from then, I began to withdraw. I didn't see my friends all that often. My social circles diminished. My tennis skills and interest started to deteriorate rapidly. I skipped sessions, practice, training, exercise. I started missing them regularly. You'd get punished for that; they'd make you train extra hard next time to the point where you passed out or vomited. They had me run in a sandpit for hours, or up Heartbreak Hill until I did actually puke! It really was like a military regime.

It got to the point where I was thinking some very unhealthy thoughts. "My parents have left me here. No one likes me. The coaches, while they'd stood up for me, seemed not to care about me anymore."

Also, I wasn't eating well. I'd discovered fast food—that great American institution!—burgers and pizza and eating vast amounts of meat. That was undoubtedly contributing to my spiral.

Meanwhile, the bullies had grown in number and become more insidious in their methods. For example, the tennis courts were all conjoined, so if I was playing on one court, any number of these bullies could be playing or just loitering in the court right beside me. They would constantly say things, whisper insults, take jibes at me, which did my game no favours. No one seemed to catch them doing it. And it would only have made things a lot worse if I'd said anything to anyone.

Things went from bad to worse. My tennis started to slip. I was sliding down the ladder. The Chinese guy I was living with decided that tennis wasn't for him and returned to China. It was decided that I should remain in that room by myself. At first, I thought this was perfect, but I was soon to find that it would only make me even more lonely and introverted.

Socially, I became very disengaged. I stopped attending the 6 a.m. fitness sessions. Sometimes I'd skip school. Sometimes I'd skip tennis; I'd fake an injury and stay in my room. I wouldn't go out. I skipped breakfast pretty much every day from year two onwards, and sometimes even skipped lunch. I wouldn't talk to anyone. I just locked myself in the room.

By the second half of my second year at the academy, I had dropped to the bottom of the tennis ladder. Everything had ground to a halt. I was going nowhere, and no one seemed to know or care.

That second year was probably one of the hardest years because that's when my mind was starting to race. I was just surrounding myself with myself. I would rearrange my room every week just to feel like it was a new place, for just a change of scenery. I'd move the bed and think, "I've got a new home now!"

But I became very aloof; even during our one-hour break, I didn't really go out. So now, on the odd occasion that I did venture out, I would be judged for it. People would say, "Oh my god, he's finally come out!" In hiding myself away, I'd made a spectacle of myself. It was a vicious cycle, because then I was even less likely to leave my room.

I didn't know what mental health was. I didn't know what psychological help was. I didn't know what psychology was. No one mentioned it, and I didn't even know that I could have probably benefitted from talking to someone. There was one point when my fitness coach pulled me into an office room and spat in my face. He was just yelling, "You're nothing! Who do you think you are, just skipping training and throwing away matches?" It was true, I would just throw matches away. But he didn't need to say what he said. He told me that I would be nothing, I would amount to nothing. So now I was being bullied from a new quarter, from the people who should have been looking out for me. Okay, I wasn't toeing the line, but his response was not helpful and couldn't have helped to fix the situation.

Worst of all was that I knew I would be disappointing my parents. I'm letting them down, and now I'm definitely not going to make it in tennis. I'd completely lost interest in it. I'd lost interest in everything. I was asking myself why I was even there at the academy anymore. However, at the same time I didn't want to go back to Nigeria because I'd be in deep shit. I was stuck. What I needed to hear was that sometimes you will not be okay, and that is okay. No matter how much we want to be strong, there will be times when the challenges in our lives are a bit too much. Be compassionate with yourself. It is okay to be down every now and then, but get professional help if you need it.

I started doing things like breaking my tennis racquet on court. I also swore a lot. Not in English, though, so I got away with it. In my first year at the academy, I learned all sorts of swear words from kids from other countries; Polish, German, Chinese, etc. I would be constantly cursing because I'd never cursed in my life; it was a new thing for me! I became addicted to it.

But whenever I broke my racquet, I'd get kicked out of the match, I'd get thrown out by the tennis coaches. So, I had a very bad attitude. I was very rough. I would tank matches; not even win a game, just 6–0, 6–0. Most times, deep down, I knew I could have won if I'd wanted to. But I was just letting it all go.

Perhaps owing to my state of mind, when I returned to Nigeria for Christmas at the end of that dreadful second year, I somehow managed to lose my visa from my passport. So when it was time to return to Texas, the authorities told me they were not able to issue me with another one. My visa was related to that particular school, the one attached to the academy. The only solution, so they told my parents, was to get another visa from a different school. And so I ended up doing my third year at the academy from a Catholic school about an hour away from my dormitory.

I can only say that I hated that school. I hated the seemingly endless commute (how quickly I'd forgotten about the go-slow!), and I hated being the odd one out again. A Hindu surrounded by Catholics! It didn't work. And so, once again, I misbehaved. I tanked it. I'd fall asleep during class, during religious instruction; worst of all, I would fall asleep during mass. That's when the teacher started saying, "Right, that's strike one!" Which he should never have done because that made me ask myself: What happens after the third strike? Would I be out?

Alas, I would never find out. I only managed to get to two strikes by the end of the year. And so for the fourth year, I was put into what they called "home school", which was run not, as you might expect, in a house, but in a nearby shopping mall.

Study was particularly self-focussed at this "home school". You sat and read on your own time, on your own schedule. Better still, there was a food court nearby. I was in there with an Egyptian and a Jamaican. Which is to say that by my last year, I had gone from a public school to a private school to kind of a home school in a shopping centre.

And would you believe it, my grades soared at Blessed Hope. That place really lived up to its name! I think that was down to the fact that the learning was autonomous. I did my work and then was free to do whatever I wanted. In a way, for the first time I was the master of my own time. I'd just wander through the shopping centre. I wouldn't sit there in class. I'd get out among the people. Which is where I've always liked to be, where I've always thrived. So I would just wander off. I'd go into a clothing shop or go to a video game arcade. And then I'd come back, read some notes, and then head off again; maybe go to the food court, eat some Chinese (I loved Chinese food at the time). My grades were many times better than when I'd been in a traditional classroom. At Blessed Hope, I thrived with a GPA of very close to 4.0.

Meanwhile, I was still playing tournaments. I was travelling the world. I played in the Philippines, Australia, India, Africa and America. I was playing a lot. Most of the global tournaments were during the summer break. That's when I'd go back to Nigeria, use that as my base, and then get sent out to all these tournaments, because during my time at the academy I was more or less full-time in school. Mostly I'd just play weekend tournaments somewhere in the United States.

My presence at these global tournaments saw my ranking start to climb once again, but this time it was my international adult ranking, not just my under-18 one. To be honest, at the academy my tennis was so-so, but when I came home and then played my tournaments, I was much better.

My ranking started to have a number: top 5,000 in the world, then 3,000, then 1,000. It was slowly climbing, and I was winning some prize money, but not enough.

All this time, I was compartmentalizing, separating all the different aspects of my life, all of my problems. I became quite adept at this. When I was in Nigeria, I completely deleted America from my mind. I removed all negative feelings, thoughts about bullies, or whatever I was going through. I would just focus on my parents, getting pampered, playing tennis tournaments, or just doing my thing as a kid.

And when I went to the US, I would act as if I didn't have parents at all, as though I was a solo person doing my own thing and living my own life. I was able to detach myself. In America I could say to myself,

"Okay. It's time to be in isolation, time to get picked on, time to do this day-by-day and get closer to graduating and getting the hell out of here."

To this day, I believe that America both broke me and made me. I joke with my dad that if I'd never gone to America, I'd be a professional tennis player today. But I would not be the more rounded person that I am today. I would still be a spoiled brat throwing tantrums and breaking racquets. America slapped some humility into me, self-development, self-discipline, self-learning, and resilience. Those four years in the academy taught me that you've got to fend for yourself, not everyone's going to like you, you are different and you've got to accept that, and there's going to be people coming after you all the time and you've got to be ready to swat them away like flies, or bring them to you in a way that they don't infect you or bite you. That's what America taught me. Which is a way of saying that being in America taught me—or at least helped to nurture—the very useful art of compartmentalization.

Lesson 4: Compartmentalization

As a young professional I often get asked how I deal with the myriad pressures, people, challenges, family pressures, or finding balance amid a hectic professional life. What they're really asking is how I deal with all these things, all at once. There's never only one thing going on in any of our lives. It's always a juggling act.

Psychology defines compartmentalization as a defence mechanism or coping strategy, which doesn't have a very good connotation. Put simply, it's how our minds deal with conflicting internal standpoints simultaneously. Coping strategies are short-term solutions, and they have positive and negative aspects. You want to compartmentalize the various events in your life, but not push them out completely.

The trick is to isolate any one issue from all the other challenges you are dealing with in your daily life. Apply extreme focus on each compartment, but only for a short period of time. You'll want to move forward in incremental steps, to move each issue along a step. You don't have to solve the whole thing in one go. Just a step at a time. Once you see progress, close the compartment and open the next one. Be careful to say "no" to things that don't deserve a compartment, that don't deserve your full attention. There's no point cluttering your mind with junk!

So those are the three steps: open, focus on, and then close the compartment. Here's a visual representation of compartmentalization: pretend that everything you're dealing with in your life is a room in a large house where you walk in and solve an equation on a white board. You have a countdown clock with less than an hour to move the problem along a single step in the right direction, after which you shut the door and move into another room equally as important. Spend your time going from compartment to compartment.

University: Take One

I left the academy after four years, a bit wiser and very weary. I wanted a year off, but my parents had other ideas. I returned to Nigeria reluctantly, and spent a year trying to slowly extricate myself from my obligations towards tennis and my parents. I didn't want to be a professional tennis player. I didn't want to live in Nigeria. And so I spent a year travelling the world, playing many tournaments, winning some, but losing a great many. My heart just wasn't in it anymore. More and more, the idea of university was popping into my head, until one day I said to my parents, "I don't think I'm a good enough player to make it to the top. I want to focus my efforts elsewhere. I want to go to university."

With my tennis ranking—I had just broken the top 1,000 worldwide— and an average SAT score, I managed to secure an academic and athletic scholarship at a very small university in Newberry, South Carolina. That was my ticket out of Nigeria. There was a catch, of course. I had to represent the college in tennis. But I'd enrolled as a Computer Science major (no idea why I picked it, except I wanted to be like Bill Gates and get rich) and was hoping that would become a way for me to slowly divert my focus.

I lasted less than five minutes in my first IT class, Java Programming. It was clear from the outset, as soon as he walked in, that the lecturer was not my cup of tea. He was all over the place (Albert Einstein-like). He just started writing on the blackboard. I couldn't handle it. It was just wrong. So after five minutes, I packed up my stuff and left.

I had an academic advisor, a very elegant and gay old man who loved to do Michael Jackson dances when he entered our classroom, which was one of my experiences with him. He was my guide.

He said, "All right. So what do you want to do?" I didn't know what I wanted to do. I thought about my dad, and said, "Oh, I guess I'll major in business." He said, "Are you sure?" I said, "Of course!" As it happened, he looked after the business faculty, so it was right up his alley. He was a bit hesitant, not about my abilities to cope with the course, more simply because I'd made the decision so quickly. But I was adamant, even though I didn't know anything about what they taught in business school. I just sort of opened my mouth and the word "business" came out of it. So that was it. That was probably one of the first moments that defined my career.

I have a lot to thank him for, because he went the extra mile with me. For example, in my first year at business school, he said to me, "I'm banning you from taking any business classes for the entire first year." I couldn't believe what I was hearing. But he clearly had a plan for me. He told me, "You're going to take left-field classes. I want you to enrol in public speaking." Can you imagine, me in public speaking?! Still, I went along with it. Another one he wanted me to do was take religion and study the Bible; being a Christian college, it was pretty clear which Bible I'd be studying. Even when I told him that I was Hindu—and all the while I was reflecting on my experiences at the Catholic school some two years before—he told me that that was what studying at college was about: broadening your horizons. I didn't have to change my faith or anything, just read and learn. He had me take art, English literature, and even photography. I was heading for a very rounded education.

I was hoping to simply glide through university but unconsciously, I was exposing myself to various topics that were quite random, and it was just semester one. Semester two was graphic design, more religion, painting in watercolour. I was learning about things I'd never took much time to think about before.

In a similar way to my early schooling, I established significant bonds with all my lecturers. It wasn't calculated; I was just interested in talking with them, learning from them. It seemed to me that not many students really got to know their teachers. But I would take the time to be collegial, say hi, and chat. In that way, they would share even more things with me and help guide my path through university.

The public speaking class was by far the toughest for me, but also—perhaps because of that—the most rewarding. I remember walking into the first class. I was absolutely terrified. Also, it was a class full of girls; I was the only guy. The lecturer said, "There are six speeches in this class, and you'll be assessed on each. The final exam is an impromptu speech, and you will be filmed while giving each speech."

I still have the video cassette of my first speech. It's somewhere in my parents' home in India. I came in sweating like Niagara Falls. I felt that I was an absolute disgrace to my class. I was *so* nervous. I was certain I was making a fool of myself. But apparently, according to others in the class, as well as the lecturer, I nailed it. That encouragement saved me in that class, because the next time I was a bit more calm; you can see that progression in the videos of the subsequent talks. By the end you can't tell if I'm sweating or not!

The lesson I took from this episode is this: *Nobody cares if you fail.* I didn't really need to be so nervous, didn't need to sweat it so much. Remember: your biggest critic is yourself. Stop worrying about what other people think—the truth is that they mostly don't think about your successes and failures at all. They're too busy thinking about themselves! It may seem depressing, but it's actually quite freeing. You're free to try, experiment, fail, try again—nobody cares anyway, so have fun! You're free to wing it and see what happens!

I thrived in those non-business classes because they were more experience-based; they weren't only about book learning and parroting facts and figures. They were more about performance. They also involved interacting with the lecturer, at least for me. My advisor really did me a favour, because these classes built up my confidence little by little. Had I gone straight into the business classes and followed a more traditional route, I might have dropped out of university altogether.

Frat Boys

By this time, I'd started playing tennis again. I'd had a frustrating previous 12 months; I was over tennis, I didn't want to play anymore, but was compelled to do the international circuit. I didn't want to play, and I didn't want to be in Nigeria. I suppose my need to get out of Lagos won in the end, because I took this scholarship, which involved me being on the university tennis team. But my life was changing, and I was okay with picking up a racquet again. Now, my routine would be university work in the morning and tennis in the afternoon. The fact that I could be social whenever I wanted helped; it could make each day feel different.

Till this point I'd had zero to do with college fraternities. They're a big thing in the U.S., but I didn't even know what one was. One of the tennis players on my team was in a fraternity. We became good friends and one day he said that he'd like to introduce me to his frat brothers. It was the first time I'd heard someone talk about a fraternity. I just though he meant they were his friends. I was to learn that they were like a little college version of the mafia!

He did indeed introduce me to his frat brothers. The first time was at the cafeteria. It turned out the frat had their own seating arrangement, had their own area. I remember taking a seat with them and being introduced to the table. I was very quiet; I just listened and said hello where necessary. Also, I was the only Indian in that group. It was basically white and African-American students that made up 99.99% of that university. So I kind of stood out everywhere, but especially in that group. They all seemed to know me as a tennis player, but I didn't know that was a big deal. I was to find out that tennis opened a lot of doors for me at that college.

I joined them at lunches and dinners, and to be honest it felt rather special that they were including me. They were asking me questions and including me. And, you know what, I became interested in them, in joining their fraternity. I learned a key lesson here: To be interesting, be interested. Show interest. It's not just okay to ask questions, it's *necessary*. Ask more questions. When someone shares something, say "Tell me more." Don't just act curious, *be curious*. The lesson I learned was to show real interest in people.

Then one day at the cafeteria, one of the boys tapped me on the shoulder and said, "Expect an envelope under your door tonight." It was very cloak-and-dagger, very secret society, mafia sort of stuff. What sort of envelope, I wondered? A letter? A wad of cash? Seriously, I had no idea.

That evening, *three* envelopes were pushed under the door! I read them slowly, several times. It seemed I was being invited to "bid" to join the fraternity. My roommate at the time was a huge guy (let's call him Brian), and he told me what it was. They wanted me to join them officially. But I would have to go through a sort of initiation.

There was a tradition whereby those who wanted to join a fraternity stood at the top of a hill on campus grounds, all lined up together. At the bottom of this particular hill was a fountain, around which were huddled the main members of the various fraternities. Those who'd received envelopes would run down this hill as fast as they could towards the fraternity they wanted to join

And did I run? Oh, I ran all right! We had an audience cheering us on, shouting and singing and waving. It was quite the spectacle, quite an event on the college calendar. I ran as fast as I could towards my chosen fraternity. They were all waiting for me at the bottom of this hill. I was fast and fit because of all the tennis. I had it in the bag; I was going to be admitted to the fraternity without any troubles at all. I was whistling through the crowd, and it really felt like they were cheering for me and me alone; or, at least, that's what I pictured. As the frat guys came closer into view, I could see they were cheering me on, sort of waving me in, happy to see me. This was great; I was already having a lot of fun. And when I got there, I gleefully received some high fives and pats on the back, when they suddenly proceeded to lift me up and chuck me right into the fountain. Which, to put it mildly, was a bit of a shock!

That was the first part of the initiation. This was followed by the obligatory lathering of shaving cream, from head to toe. This was the start of my fraternity journey.

Apparently, it was considered a privilege to be invited to make a bid. I didn't realize that. A lot of it no doubt had to do with me being a tennis player. What I would come to realize was that when you play athletics in America, you are treated quite differently from the non-sporting people; you get invited to all sorts of events, lecturers love you, and you get all kinds of special treatment.

Something I've come to notice in my life is that friends come and go, and that's alright. I've met many, many people in my 39 years. I have learned that sometimes the ephemeral friendships—the ones that last one year, one week, or even one evening—can be as transformational as the long-term ones. Instead of regretting the loss of some friends, I'm grateful I got to learn from them in the first place.

So it was nice to be making all these new friends. But my membership in the frat came with expectations. We were all often challenged to do things, often stupid things. Not unusual for college. Some of which included a challenge to drink a 48-pack of beer. I had to either finish the pack or drink until I passed out. I think I made it to 12 or 14 before puking everywhere. Other challenges included doing everyone's dirty laundry, toilet-papering the Dean's house which was nearby the campus—and not just a bit of the house, almost every inch of it, including down the chimney, everywhere!—doing assignments for other people, dancing with girls at parties; horrible, clownish things that were humiliating for everyone. All in a bid to be allowed to join the fraternity.

But I did my bidding, and eventually got in. And all of a sudden I was not excluded anymore, not seen as an outsider. I was protected by my brothers, and the sorority sisters loved us.

I still didn't have a girlfriend, by the way. I hadn't really spoken to many girls at all. Some did approach me as an athlete, but I pushed them all away. I was too awkward, too nervous.

But after joining the frat, my social life skyrocketed. I remember passing out in a bush which happened to be in front of the economics building, and of all people, the professor who was acting as my mentor found me there as he was walking in to take his class. A class that I was supposed to be in! I must have fallen asleep at some point just before dawn. It was now about 8:30 a.m., and the class was to start at 9 a.m.

He said, "Oh, Mr. Sridhar!" (He always called me Mr. Sridhar.) "Are you planning on coming to class this morning?" I think he had to give me a bit of a prod to wake me up. He said again, "Are you coming to macroeconomics?" I remember looking up at him with the sun behind his towering frame, bringing stinging tears to my no doubt bloodshot eyes. I mumbled something in agreement, telling him that yes, of course, I was coming to class, I absolutely had every intention of being there!

Despite all the socializing I was doing, my grades were good. I think my brain shifted as a result of being exposed to a diverse range of classes; I found it quite easy to pick things up, even if I wasn't in the best shape at the time.

As I mentioned, I was taking classes like watercolours, graphic design, and photography, and soon found I'd completed most of the courses required for a degree in art. I actually ended up getting a double degree, in business and art. It excited me, being a bit creative, not being beholden to formulas and numbers. Meanwhile, I was also taking calculus and trigonometry. In terms of the numbers-related courses, and the business courses, I was doing reasonably well there too. But, to be honest, it was the other stuff that really excited me.

Break Point

While my education was going swimmingly, as was my social life, my tennis began to suffer. Although I hadn't exactly fallen back in love with it after my year on the international circuit, I'd not been wholly against playing when I started in South Carolina. But as other things began to take over, the old resentment towards playing started creeping back into my game.

There was one particular match that summed up my whole attitude at the time. We were playing a college in North Carolina. My coach had obviously noticed that my motivation had been slipping, but so far he hadn't really said anything. He was usually a pretty quiet sort of person. An observer, I think, like me. And no doubt he'd seen my temper get the better of me. The outbursts, the swearing, broken racquets; but he'd also seen me winning matches when it seemed like I couldn't win. So on one side, he was seeing talent, and on the other side he was seeing an idiot. Which no doubt would have been frustrating for a coach. But to his credit, until now he hadn't let any of that frustration show.

We needed to win against North Carolina in order to secure the championship. But they were very good, and it was almost an impossible task. It was unlikely we'd beat them.

It was doubles first and then singles. To our amazement, by the time we got to the end, to the last match, my match, it was all tied up at four wins each. The winner of my match would decide who won the day and hence the championship.

I lost the first set resoundingly 6–2. It was far from a good start. But I managed to come back, winning the next one 6–4 in my favour.

In the third set I was winning 5–0, I was in the clear. But then my other side started to come out. I lost one point, one measly point, and despite being ahead by some margin I threw a tantrum. I chucked my racquet up into the nearby gazebo. I'm four points from winning the match, but still I throw this tantrum for losing the point. The score was love–15, but when the umpire saw me throw the racquet, he called a point penalty for my poor behaviour. So that took it to love–30.

At receiving the point penalty, I lost it completely and swore at the umpire, called him every name under the sun. Which, (surprise, surprise), did me no favours at all. This time it wasn't a point penalty, but a game penalty. So the score went to 5–1.

I was still way ahead. All I had to do was win one game and I'd win the match, the university would win the championship. The trouble was, if I made one more discretion, one more outburst, and I wouldn't lose any more points, I would lose the entire match.

At this point, I could sense how angry and nervous our coach is. But all I had to do was win four more points.

He came to the side of the fence and called me over. All of a sudden he was seeing red. He said to me, "Kaushik, if you fuck this up, I'm going to cut your scholarship and you will be eliminated from the university."

You'd think that would have been enough for me to put my head down and get the job done. Unfortunately, I still had a bit to learn. His words did not refocus me, did not calm me down or help me see reason. They had what we might call the opposite effect. I was yet to learn a very important skill when it came to focus and determination, something that is useful in sports, business and life in general, and it's something I like to call The Switch.

Lesson 5: The Switch

All great athletes have a mental switch, and it should be your goal to get one too. Think of a light switch in your house. You flip it, and the lights turn on. Pretty simple, right? Well, a mental switch is in your brain. When you flip it, your mind goes to a state of perfect concentration, intensity, and confidence.

The most experienced athletes usually have effective, powerful mental switches. They can make themselves internally sharp with a snap of their fingers, just by recognizing that they've got a job to do and it's time to get it done. They can be having a conversation and a few laughs, and in a matter of a few seconds they're ready to rock and roll. They recognize the task in front of them, and apply the right level of inner strength to it. Then, after they've taken care of business, they can flip the switch off and relax.

Manipulating your attention is key to flipping the switch. By moving from being distracted and taking in the world around you to narrowing your vision on one task, the full weight of your mind's abilities get behind you. Over the course of my tennis career, I learned to narrow my attention, to focus on the person ahead of me and the goal at hand.

Finally, great athletes know how to turn that switch off. Research on elite athletes shows that resiliency is tied to efficient termination of the stress response. In other words, once the competition is over, or once they've utilized their turbo switch, they turn it off. Either saving it for later or transitioning into recovery mode. This oft-neglected skill prevents the problem of over-competing, or when you lose the effectiveness of being able to compete because competing becomes the norm. Like a coffee addict who no longer feels the effect of caffeine, you lose the ability to flip the switch when it matters most.

Break Point (Continued)

I was now so angry, that I lost the next four games just to spite my coach. Terrible, I know. A horrible showing. But I wanted to show him that I was in control of this, not him.

So the games were now level at 5–5. No doubt my coach was thinking about how he's going to give me the boot come Monday. I lost another game and it's now 5–6. All my opponent had to do now was win four points and that whole shebang goes to them.

But somehow I managed to flip a switch and get myself back on course. I got my head back in the game, despite the distractions off-court. The match went to a tiebreaker and I ended up winning 10–6. Everyone was relieved, everyone was happy. My coach didn't say anything.

Unfortunately, that wasn't the end of it. Whenever I played in those days, I didn't stretch, nor did I stay very hydrated. My warmups weren't always the best. On this particular day it was very hot and humid. Nevertheless, I didn't think too much about it. We all piled into a van and our coach drove us off to get pizza. But after we arrived at the pizza place, I got out of the van and simply collapsed. I had a full body cramp because I was so dehydrated. It was a pain like you wouldn't believe. After a moment of writhing around on the ground, I passed out.

When I regained consciousness, there was an ambulance beside me and a couple of medics trying to get me to sign something. But my cramps were so bad that I could barely hold the pen, and even while I was lying down I was seeing stars. I stayed there by the highway for a long time, but eventually I was okay. I got up and still managed to go inside and have pizza!

Despite my episode, my coach still let his feelings be known. He questioned whether or not I was invested in tennis, whether I really wanted to win. The old ambivalence returned, only this time I felt at liberty to tell him. It was clear for him to see that my heart wasn't in it, and I thought he'd cut my scholarship and send me packing back to Nigeria for sure. What I didn't anticipate was that, unbeknownst to me, he was quitting at the end of that term, which likely meant that he was the one who wasn't invested in the team. It was likely his looming departure that meant I was able to stay on the team and retain my scholarship.

It was because of this, because I'd been let off the hook, that life for me plateaued and I found myself cruising along at Newberry University. That's not to say I was doing well in all areas, far from it, but I managed to slip back into my old habits of keeping to myself, shutting out other people, eating take-away junk food and staying up all night watching television. My grades were good, and my tennis was average. I didn't have a passion for much, and if I was honest with myself, I couldn't really see where I wanted to go in the future. Which is to say I didn't have much of an identity.

In fact, I still don't have an identity. I can't say exactly where I'm from. It's a bit from here, a bit from there, and another bit from over there. I can't speak my official language; I don't know where I am. I just kind of go with the flow. I always have.

I had all sorts of different names at university. People had trouble pronouncing my actual name and came up with others to compensate. My coach called me Kal as in Kal Penn (from *Superman*), someone else called me Cash Money, and others still called me Shik-dog. So I just went with the flow; I was fine with whatever people wanted to call me. I never reacted negatively or aggressively.

Even today, my dad says to me, "You're too easy-going. You're not a serious guy. You're never serious!"

I suppose, if I was serious, I'd be at a different level now. I'd be an executive, a CEO or a Top 100 professional tennis player. But I just didn't care all that much; I always internalized things. I was more concerned about today. I didn't much think about tomorrow.

After almost four years, graduation was looming. I had absolutely no plans for the future, nothing in mind for who or where I wanted to be. I didn't even have a visa to remain in the States, so I had to come up with something pretty quickly! And one day, three months before graduation, it came to me: I should become a tennis coach.

I'd seen what my coach at the time was doing; I'd seen what other coaches had done in the past. They seemed to have pretty good lives. I thought to myself, "Yes, I can do that."

I looked up the requirements for the United States Professional Tennis Association (USPTA). In order to qualify as a coach, you had to do written test and then conduct a coaching lesson. This was where my "Nigerian brain" came out. I called my dad and said, "You know that club where I play in Lagos, every time I come home?" I'd built some good bonds with the coaches there. So I said to Dad, "Can you get me a letter from that club with their letterhead saying I've been a coach with them for X number of years?" I think this appealed to my dad's natural out-of-the-box thinking. Dad sorted it for me, and I soon had my letter.

The closest place to take the exam was Hilton Head, South Carolina. After I applied, they sent me this whopping great folder. I must admit, I only read about five pages. I though to myself, "I know how to hit a good forehand. I don't need a manual to tell me that." I closed it, got in my car, and booked a hotel room in Hilton Head. I didn't realize I was heading to one of the dodgiest suburbs in South Carolina. Still, I arrived on a Friday night, checked in to the hotel, which was surrounded by any number of unseemly characters. I'd never been alone like this before, staying in a hotel and doing my own thing. So, of course, I went to a famous burger chain restaurant, grabbed a few burgers and just stayed in my room.

The next morning, I sat for the exam. It was like an SAT exam. I felt that I did reasonably well; it was all common sense. This was on Saturday.

On Sunday, I had to conduct a lesson. Bear in mind, I'd never taught tennis to anyone before. I'd played it, a lot of it, but I'd never taught it.

Still, I had confidence. I just felt that I could nail it, and that I was going to nail it. It was the same mentality I took into university exams. These days, even my wife says I'm weird to behave in this way. I love job interviews. I look forward to job interviews. It's one of my favourite things in the world, getting a job interview. In a similar way, I used to love doing exams, because I knew I was going to be on top. This might sound odd but exam week was my favourite week in the year. I loved that pressure.

That Sunday, I fronted with only my racquet. I wasn't dressed very well. (Despite the less than salubrious area, the country club was very excusive.) I think I was wearing track pants and a top. They told me I'd be taking charge of two lessons that day. First, it would be a group of kids, followed by a one-on-one with a pro.

Not only had I never taught a lesson before, I'd never interacted with kids before. But I went with the flow. They gave me a basket of balls and told me I had an hour. I didn't skip a beat. It was in my nature to wing it!

The key, I figured, was to create a good atmosphere. That was the most important thing; technique was a distant second. So I introduced myself to the kids and started playing around with them, got them running about, then started tossing balls to them. After I started to get into the swing of things, I started setting myself goals. If I could get them to hit one good ball, if one shot went over the net, I would feel that the lesson had been a success. And they did it.

The kids had a great time. That was my main focus. If they had a great time and failed to hit the ball over the net, then so be it; at least they'd have had fun. This was a lot different to the approach I'd been subjected to as a child. But they had an absolutely great time.

Then I had the pro. I lowered my ego now. I felt that it was more important to make him look good, make him feel confident. I was more serious now, and focussed on technique through a number of rallies. The assessors saw that I could make a lesson fun when required, but could also keep it serious. I didn't have this plan to begin with; I simply let it unfold as the day rolled on. I just winged it.

I felt that it went well. But now it was out of my hands. I had to let them decide. Bear in mind, this was the USPTA; these are the people who coached Pete Sampras and Andre Agassi. I knew it was going to be tough.

But I finished my exams and returned to the Newberry campus. I had a sinking feeling going back, for my life had stagnated and I was on the verge of descending into another dark patch. I was feeling shy and nervous, and I'd started sweating a lot. Oddly enough, when I did that coaching it had been over 30 degrees, but I didn't sweat. I'd noted it at the time, and it was the first time I'd realized that the sweating problem was psychological.

To my relief, I got the email from the USPTA two days later. I was certified. Not only that, I was level one. That was just one rung below someone who coached Roger Federer.

Of course, classic Kaushik, I had no idea what I was going to *do* with this qualification. All I'd thought about until then was getting it. Now that I had it, I had to use it. To tide me over, I'd applied for a job at a global credit card company in South Carolina. I certainly didn't want this job, in fact I was dreading it, but I needed a job and this was the pick of a fairly uninspiring bunch.

Then, one night not long before I was due to start with the company, I was woken by a phone call at 3 a.m. It was someone calling from Australia. She had checked the database of certified coaches and discovered my profile and playing history. She said, "I'm building a tennis school in Albury. Would you be interested in coming to Albury and building my tennis school with me?"

The first thing I said was, "Where the hell's Albury?!"

"New South Wales," she said.

"Where is New South Wales?" I said.

"In Australia,' she said.

"I have spent time in Australia," I said, recalling a tournament I'd played in Darwin.

It all sounded promising, but I needed to think about it. I told her I'd get back to her. The next morning, I called my parents and told them about the tennis school in Albury. They were reasonable; they asked me what I wanted to do. What *did* I want to do? In that moment, something clicked and I saw this as an opportunity to escape having to find a corporate job in America. I thought I wanted a simpler life, and coaching seemed a way to have that.

When the person from Albury called again, they asked to see some videos of me coaching people. Now, although the record books might have showed that I had been coaching for many years, in reality I had never coached anyone. Nevertheless, I said "Oh yes, of course, I'll send you something!"

This was right before I graduated from Newberry, which I did summa cum laude because while my personal and tennis lives had taken a downward turn, my academic performance had remained strong. It was all very satisfying, and I received accolades from my friends and frat brothers, which was something that I was surprisingly moved by. It's still such a pleasant memory.

But I had a coaching film to make. No time to bask in glory. After graduation, I flew back to Lagos. Almost as soon as I landed, we'd organized everything. My dad had organized a small film crew, and we went to my country club, where my usual coach would play my student, and the Nigerian ball boys became the group of kids that I coached. Some real Steven Spielberg stuff. Still, I wanted to make it work. I wanted this to happen. Little did I know, the outcome of this film would have a tremendous impact on my life and the direction it would take. In the end, we got it done and shipped the video off to Albury. We must have done something right; before long I received yet another call from them saying they liked what they saw, and so began my life's next chapter in Australia.

Part Three

Australia

Learning to Fly

The thing is, I don't like being institutionalized, I don't like that sort of thinking. In my life, whenever things looked like they were going in a more conventional direction—whether it's being a tennis pro, an academic, or a member of the corporate world—I've always shied away from it. I like lateral thinking; I like things that come out of left field. I enjoy being kept on my toes.

I don't think anyone thought I'd be a tennis coach, certainly not my parents. They just thought I'd play college tennis, get a degree in business and art and become a businessman. But here I was, continuing in the tennis world.

I was happy because, after all these years playing tennis, I wanted some return on everything I'd invested. So becoming a coach was ticking two boxes: giving me a return on investment, and getting me into a new country, a new chapter. Otherwise, I'd have seen my tennis career as a complete waste. The progress I'd made, the ranking and the money, all that didn't really mean much to me. But after university I felt I needed to build upon what I'd started, while also allowing for an out of left field change. So I came to Albury, and I thought, "This is a new life, this is a new chapter, while also being so random." I suppose that's what coming to Albury was: a sudden turn, a leap of faith.

And it was a leap of faith for everyone, I think. The academy I was joining was a start-up enterprise. They were bringing me into the fold during the very early stages of the business. So while it was a great opportunity for me in terms of getting a coaching career going, it was also a great opportunity to help build a business and see how these things work from the ground up.

To be honest, I could never have grown into what I am today if I'd stayed in Albury. But I feel that it was essential for my evolution, and I'm very grateful for the opportunity, because that job made me who I am today, in terms of communication. I was going into an academy that wasn't built; it needed a lot of stakeholder engagement. It needed a lot of grassroots thinking regarding how to build a business.

Now, I'd never done any of that. But again, it was going to teach me how to wing it, how to bring dollars in, how to build a website, to market the tennis academy, how to communicate with three-year-olds to 82-year-olds.

For the first few months, I was just winging it. I made up the classes as I went along. One of the owners of the academy helped me get settled into an apartment (which was roughly the size of two bathrooms joined together) and bought me a bicycle so I could ride to the academy each morning. I was lost, didn't know anyone, didn't even know really if coaching was the right thing for me, but I was calm, I wasn't stressed about it.

Initially, I taught both at the tennis club and a nearby school. In the mornings it was always up to the school, where I ran the lessons on a basketball court. Each morning I would ride to the tennis club, get the net and the balls, walk over to the school and teach the kids for a few hours. That was before breakfast. After breakfast, it was private lessons at the court then home for lunch. Then the after-school program would run from 2 p.m. to 6 p.m.

To begin with, I absolutely loved it. I loved the interactions with all the different people more than the actual tennis. I really enjoyed teaching so many different people. It was a learning experience for me as well, because at one time you may be teaching four-year-olds (under the watchful eyes of their demanding parents), who could barely even walk, let alone swing a racquet, so I had to develop ways to engage them and communicate with them.

Meanwhile, the owner of the academy would invite me to her home. She had a daughter who I adored and she adored me in return.

Once again, my diet was terrible: absolute junk. The nearby post office had this amazing banana-flavoured milk. I became addicted to those! I was exposed to a few things in Albury: banana milk, burgers with pineapple on them. Classic, Australian cuisine! Every day, I would go and buy a sandwich and a burger, a banana milk, and few other things. I'll be the first to admit, it was pretty disgusting.

One day, I was put in charge of travelling to regional areas in order to drum up a bit more business, securing contracts with other schools and clubs. For which, naturally, I would need a car. I'd had a car in the States, but obviously that was no good to me in Australia, being a left-hand drive. The people at Service New South Wales gave me a P plate, and I bought a Commodore station wagon in which I could carry all my equipment all over the countryside. (My driving left more than a little to be desired, and I managed to get myself into the odd scrape every now and then!)

I visited so many country towns, places that I had absolutely no idea existed on this planet. Tiny towns of 100-200 people, each of which had its own school. I'd go to these schools, talk to the principals and somehow win contracts.

Every day, if I was not teaching in Albury, I'd be hitting the countryside to some of the remotest towns. I was seeing a lot of the lesser-known areas of Australia. It was a great introduction to Australian culture.

Regardless of who I was talking to, I would try to connect with them via a story. Often I would use a story about my background or my time at the Academy. I always looked for a thread. I was able to weave a story that connected with the other person, and then the rest was easy.

I drove quite a long way to teach in these towns. I loved the kids I taught, and I think the kids loved me because I was not impatient, I was not into yelling. I was always smiling and very relaxed.

That's not to say I was a complete pushover. I could get a bit tough if they kept hitting the ball into the net, if their focus or their attention span started to dip. That's when my other side would come out, the strict parent side. I learned to be balanced.

I think the mums liked me a lot, too. Word had got around and I was receiving lots of requests for private lessons. I started winning a lot of work for the academy through those private lessons as well, but it was only the mums. Curiously, I didn't have any male students!

Meanwhile, the business wasn't doing that well. I didn't have the full picture, didn't know the budgets and spends and allocations; I was kept at a distance from that side of the business. For a variety of reasons, I sensed that things were not panning out the way the owners had hoped. Also, I felt that my work wasn't being appreciated. I was slogging, driving and winning contracts, but found that I wasn't getting any encouragement, wasn't being acknowledged or made to feel part of the team.

Sometime in those first few months, however, my boss took me to Melbourne to see my first AFL match. I remember thinking to myself, "What is this sport? It's so weird!" Because I had come from NFL and baseball in the States. AFL was just so different. It was such a surreal experience in that stadium at the time. My boss was sweet, initially, especially for those first few months. But as time went on, I think the pressures of running a business were starting to get to her.

There were a lot of moments when I questioned what exactly they were doing. Management would ask me, "Can you help build a website for the company?" I'd never done it before, but I managed to do it. So I was learning a lot of things thanks to her, like negotiation, customer service, stakeholder engagement, website design. But remember, I was the tennis coach! Surely you'd get professionals to do these sorts of things?

My diet had not improved, and I wasn't really playing tennis. I was just standing and hitting a ball or telling kids to run around, so my diet was starting to backfire for the first time. I was getting nice and round, and that started affecting me a bit. I became a slob. Things were starting to turn a bit downwards again.

At some point during that first year, my mum came to visit me. After seeing everything in the area, we decided to spend a few days in Sydney. I was excited to get out of Albury and go to a bigger city for a while. We did the usual tourist things. I clearly remember, we were on a tour bus and the driver pointed and said, "To your left is Macquarie University, the CBD campus. They have many good programs, especially their MBA." To this day, I don't know why he said that; it seemed like such a specifically random thing to note on a tourist bus. Anyway, I am glad he did!

At this juncture, it's worth noting that I was under a lot of pressure from my parents to get married. "You need to start thinking about your future. If you want to get married, you need to have a good job, you need to have a good education. And a Bachelor's degree is not enough, you need to get a Master's." These were the words that were bubbling away in the back of my mind, even if I didn't entirely agree.

But when I was on that bus and the driver said the magic word "MBA", my mum got excited, leaned over and said, "Kaushik, if you do this, you might be a lucrative prospect on the online marriage platforms in India!" Of course, I laughed it off. But, at the same time, that was a very momentous, important moment in my life, because it remained at the back of my mind: Macquarie MBA.

We returned to Albury, Mum left, and I moved houses. At last, I got a bigger apartment for myself. It was still a bit dingy, but much better than before. It was around this time that my tennis coaching started to deteriorate. I was losing interest. I was gaining weight. I was lonely again; because of my schedule, I didn't have friends. I wasn't making friends. I was not very social again. My routine was kids, come back home, then go to the owner's house. That was my little bubble.

I was making some extra money by stringing racquets (which, of course, I'd never done before, but I learned). Each day I'd spend a couple of hours in my boss's garage stringing racquets for clients. I was spending way too much time and energy on something that my heart just wasn't into. After the novelty of that first year wore off, I was back to having doubts about tennis. I loved my clients, I loved the kids I taught, but I knew, deep down, that coaching just wasn't for me.

Coaching started bringing me down. Another downward spiral was starting to unfold. This would be one of the lowest points in my life. Believe it or not, I wasn't being bullied or beaten up, I didn't have sporting or academic pressure on me. Nevertheless, I was very low. This time, my low mood manifested itself as an inability to sleep. I would come back to my home in Schubach Street, and I would just lie down staring at the ceiling, praying that I might get to sleep. This was new terrain for me. I'd never had sleep issues. "Should I count sheep? Should I count backwards? Should I do this? Should I do that?" I just couldn't sleep. And I'd fall asleep at 5 a.m., but I'd have to wake up at 6 a.m.

I knew I had to get out of Albury. I needed to stop coaching, but was very scared because I didn't know what to do with my life. Nothing was coming to me in the form of luck, chance, fate, or even a blessing. I was in the middle of nowhere. I'd grown to dislike my bosses. They were not letting me grow. My mind started to race again: I would think about my parents, ask myself what they would say. Were they going to be ashamed of me? I began to dread each new day.

And then, in typical Kaushik fashion, inspiration struck! I was maybe in the shower, or lying in bed trying to sleep, and I just thought, "Macquarie University MBA." Which was followed closely by the appealing idea of living in a big city. I'd never lived in a big city. I'd lived in San Antonio, Texas, but that was in a jungle, far, far away from San Antonio. I'd lived in South Carolina, an hour from Colombia. And now Albury. Lagos wasn't like the big city I had in my head; Lagos was just chaotic. The thought of life in the big city started to fascinate me.

Of course, in order to get into an MBA course I had to satisfy certain criteria. Firstly, I was too young. For a good Western MBA, you require a few years of experience in the field. The Macquarie website stated that they took two students in each cohort that were valedictorian where they got their degree and had two years of work experience. Once again, it was time to wing it!

I needed to get busy. I revisited my resumé, searching for anything that I could make fit the criteria. I said to myself, "There's six months here and six months there: that's *technically* work. You got paid for one and the other one ... well, what they don't know ..." I was also nearing one year as a professional tennis coach. Kate would give me the title of general manager. By my calculations, I got two years! And of course, I was valedictorian at Newberry College.

I called my parents with the good news. But I framed it like this: "You always wanted me to do an MBA, so I'm going to make your wish come true! I'll be all over those marriage websites in no time!"

Of course, it was more for me than for them. But I could hear their sighs of relief all the way from India to Albury.

So I asked my boss to write me up a letter explaining my position as General Manager. Although until then I didn't have the official GM title, I was doing all the work associated with the position: winning clients, attracting people to the academy, keeping everyone happy, and all the tasks a typical GM would do. They knew I wanted to do the MBA, and they were very nice about it, even though they knew that I would be leaving them. I think they could tell my enthusiasm had waned. And by that time the business was starting to have troubles.

After that, I emailed South Carolina and got reference letters from five of my lecturers. I got all the documentation shipped in from South Carolina, got my Albury stuff sorted, packaged it up neatly, tied it with a bow and sent it off to Sydney. Within a couple of weeks, I received an email from the Dean telling me that I had been accepted into the 2008 January cohort of their one-year MBA program.

At the time, the Macquarie MBA program was among the top 50 in the world. To be honest, I didn't rate my chances. Therefore, I also applied to the University of Queensland and Edinburgh University in Scotland. Now that I'd decided I wanted to do an MBA, I cast a wide net.

On being accepted, I sent that email to my parents. It was one of the proudest days of their lives, and thus mine. I tendered my resignation in Albury. My dad came to pack up my belongings and helped me move.

I didn't go straight to Sydney. I resigned from coaching in April 2007, but the course didn't begin until January 2008, so I knew had another eight months free to spend in India. By this time, Mum and Dad had moved back to India. They were semi-retired, but Dad was more of a consultant with the company he worked for and was flying in to Lagos for two months at a time. So India became our base. I had to keep myself occupied for eight months.

I was 23 and it had been 10 years since I'd lived full-time with my parents. I started to think, "Shit. What have I done?" Still, I'd gotten away from coaching, I'd gotten away from tennis, I'd gotten away from the downward spiral. I have not played tennis since April 2007.

Mastering Business

Albury was a hell of an experience, but it laid the foundation for being agile and adaptable for survival. No doubt I can also thank the Academy for my gift of survival, but Albury taught me about communication, and how to wing it. And I did really wing it; God knows how many conversations with school principals I'd had where I had no idea what I was going in with. And I certainly winged my job interview with the people in Albury.

I learned a lot of things in Albury that are transferable to a boardroom career. The way that I survived in that job. I'd never taught tennis before; I'd never won a contract, nor had I ever built a website. I was literally hitting KPIs as I learned them. It was all valuable experience.

I had eight months in India before starting the MBA, and I needed them. My health was poor, as was my mental state. I still wasn't sleeping well. I am very grateful to my parents for taking care of me over that time. That time in India fixed everything. I improved my sleep patterns, lost weight and built up my confidence again. It was also a time when my parents and I became really close. It was just me and them.

Throughout it all, my dad kept telling me, "Make sure you're well prepared because you're going to have a lot of work to do once you start the MBA. Make sure you're well prepared. There'll be a lot of pressure. Remember, you'll be the youngest in your year." But I didn't prepare at all. I just enjoyed my life, ate well, exercised, and I was just going to wing it. I didn't know then, how right he was.

The program consisted of four terms over the year. That was part of the appeal; usually an MBA takes two years full-time. I was already the youngest in the cohort, so I thought if I could get it done in a year, I'd be 24 and have this wonderful qualification. It would set me up. But it also meant that they compressed a lot of material into that one year.

It was a very eclectic bunch; a mix of Indians, Americans, Europeans, and Australians. It was like the Olympics in there! So many different races, which made for a great experience. It was also a much older group than I expected, most of whom were aged 35 to 55, with a fresh-faced Kaushik thrown in the mix.

To begin with, I found the material easy. The first course was Organizational Behaviour and our lecturer's name was the same as a famous and insane action Hollywood actor, and rather soft-spoken (not a leather tassel in sight!). To be honest, I was a bit bored within the first half an hour; my mind began to wander, my attention shifted to the others in the room. I started observing my classmates to see how they listened. I was wondering if they were thinking what I was thinking. To me, everything that he was saying seemed like common sense. I felt like I understood all of it pretty much immediately. It was a relief to know I wasn't out of my depth.

I moved into my on-campus accommodation. I had three flatmates, two brothers from South America, and a guy from Germany who ended up being my best friend. I introduced him to his wife at some point that year. He was very introverted, and the two Latin Americans didn't speak a lot of English, so I became their sort of conduit to the outside world. I relished this, because I could use my extroverted side to help them. I thrived on it, actually. He and I made quite the picture: he was a 34-year-old, 6'4 German, and I was a 24-year-old, 5'10 Indian! In a way, taking the social leader role of our little circle helped to bring me out of my shell too.

During that first term, there was another class called Foundations for Management Thought. It was the class with the highest failure rate in the whole MBA programme. The professor had worked in industrial psychology and as a psychotherapist. He was apparently well-renowned in the field, but to me he was a bit of an ass. Many international students would fail because of his class; they'd have to go back to their home countries because their results got cancelled.

On the first day of class he asked, "How many of you here have been managers or are managers?" Some of us raised our hands. He looked around the room and said, "You're all a bunch of idiots." I don't know if he was trying to impress or intimidate us. I just remember thinking, "Oh, is this normal or what?" He was a strange character; each week during that 10-week course, he would take on the character of a different philosopher. It was like a proper performance. Very odd. One week he would speak as Homer, then Plato or Socrates, and would teach management from that philosopher's perspective.

It certainly broadened my horizons. He would say some very controversial things, and obviously we had some outspoken, mature students who would question him, and he would just shut them down. He didn't seem to care what people thought of him or how he made people feel. He certainly wasn't politically correct. It opened my eyes to other ways of doing things, or at least seeing things, that's for sure.

Back in Organizational Behaviour, we had our first group assignment, and there was a presentation component to it. My group consisted of myself, people from Mexico, France, and a couple of others; five of us all together. Some of them were from the Department of Foreign Affairs in France. There were some heavy-hitters in that room. And then there was me, with not all that much to my name, a cobbled-together resumé and some tennis coaching experience.

The more senior people in my group were talking as if they bloody ran Microsoft. They were adamant that we'd need to do the project a certain way. They were completely overbearing, but they weren't achieving any consensus on how to divvy up the assignment. After an endless back and forth of getting nowhere, I decided to throw my hat in the ring. I said, "Guys, can I say something?" I think that works really well. I'm silent 99% of the time in a meeting, and then at the right moment I say, "Can I say something?" I find that when I say that, everyone just goes silent because they're thinking, "This guy hasn't opened his mouth. Maybe he has something that's interesting." It's a good way of interjecting effectively without having to rant and rave.

It's important to remember that patience is a powerful tool for success. No matter how much talent you have, or the iron-clad work ethic you adhere to, if you don't have patience, you will not go very far. But patience is about more than business success. It is also a key to health and happiness. Patience is an antidote to both stress and anger. Being patient allows you to overcome challenging situations in your life. This flexibility helps you to better adapt to life's inevitable curveballs.

Now, I had the floor; they were now all looking at me waiting for me to continue. I took them back to the assignment and what we needed to do in order to answer the question. Also, I knew what everyone's skills were, where they were coming from professionally. I realized that we could each bring our own expertise to the project and not have to step on each other's toes. I said to different team members, "You, you've got marketing experience. So you do this. You, you've got this experience, so you handle this," and so forth. Of course, none of them wanted to present the assignment in front of the class. They all had stage fright. But I could do it. And I knew it would bring the team together. So I said I'd do that component. That's where my skills lay. When working in a team, it's important to identify and focus in on each individual's skillset. That way, you'll be free to do what you do best, and so will the others. It's a bit like compartmentalizing, but in this case—if you think of the project as a big house—everyone's skills make up the different rooms of that house. You go away and do your work, focus on your strengths, then reconvene and collect everything together under the team moniker.

The day of the presentation came. It was held in a sort of auditorium. The speaker stood at floor-level and spoke up to the audience in banked seating. I'd designed the slides and had everything ready to go. Of course, it was not rehearsed. The material was prepared, but I was flying by the seat of my pants.

One of our group members who was a manager at one of the world's largest software companies, opened proceedings. She mumbled and fumbled a bit; I don't think she really enjoyed public speaking all that much. But it was fine. Then she handed over to me.

Ever since the very first class of that MBA year, I'd felt as though most of the cohort were looking down their noses at me. They were managers, had run their own companies, had often over 20-30 years' experience, and challenged me about my place on the program. "How did you get in?" was not an uncommon question. They were quite competitive, which often belied a lack of self-confidence. Even as I strode onto that platform to present our project, I could still feel their air of superiority hanging around like a bad smell.

Even so, I did the presentation. And I did it well, I think, because I sensed the mood in that auditorium shift. The perception of a group of people with collectively more than hundreds of years of experience, from all over the world, looked at me with different eyes–with a sort of respect (or at least acknowledgement), that I did indeed belong in the course.

From that day, the view of the cohort changed. They looked up to me, in a way, and for a number of future assessments I would always be the nominated presenter. It sort of became my thing.

One presentation has stayed with me. We had to play the role of a wine company. We had samples of wine that we were going to hand out. I really wanted to make it a unique presentation, so I started taking shots of wine. Keep in mind, this was an assessment task, for an MBA program.

I pretended to be tipsy. I was not really tipsy, but I pretended, and I used that to amuse the audience. The group would say that that was one of the most memorable presentations because there was alcohol involved. I suppose I must have learned something from a particular lecturer who adopted the roles of the great philosophers for each class, because I dropped into my role as tipsy provocateur seamlessly. I was running around the room, handing out shots, and coming back to the pointer on how this was going to be a return on investment. It was important to be on point with the numbers, the financials, while also being entertaining. The marketing professor almost fell out of his chair.

I was good at blending the social with the professional. And my social life was fun and becoming fuller by the week. There were lots of impromptu nights out, journeys around the city, to clubs and bars, to Kings Cross. It was a very social time for me, and that cohort really came together and accepted each other, for the most part. There was a core of about 10 of us, and I remember feeling empowered by the fact that I was included in it. I hosted a beer-pong party, and even dressed up in makeup and heels for Mardi-Gras! I also started going to concerts. The first one I went to was the Foo Fighters in Sydney. And over the next couple of years I would attend some 200 concerts. I thrive on the energy, and try to go to as many as I can. It was at this time that I started realizing the value of every day, every second, and that if I wanted to have a rich, fulfilling life, I'd have to view my time as a precious commodity.

Lesson 6: The Value of 86,400 seconds

"Time is very slow for those who want, very fast for those who are scared, very long for those who are sad and very short for those who celebrate but for those who love, time is eternal"

– William Shakespeare

Everyday, 86,400 seconds are deposited into your life account. These seconds are so much more powerful than money because you can always make more money, you can't always make more time.

- To realize the value of 1 year, ask a student who failed a grade
- To realize the value of 1 month, ask a parent who lost their child in the first month
- To realize the value of 1 week, ask an editor of an online magazine
- To realize the value of 1 hour, ask a couple who are in a long-distance relationship
- To realize the value of 1 minute, ask a person who just missed a bus, train or plane
- To realize the value of 1 second, ask a person who just missed an accident
- To realize the value of 1 millisecond, ask a person who just came 2nd at the Olympics.

Life and time are the two best teachers. Life teaches us to make good use of time and time teaches us the value of life. At the end of the day, once they're all used up, you get a new 86,400 seconds. We would never waste it if it was money, so why do we waste it when it comes to time? So there's both good news and bad news: The bad news is time flies. The good news is you're the pilot. The biggest mistake is you thinking that you have infinite amount of time.

Lesson 7: Existence

Time is a quality of existence. Existence has had humanity baffled for centuries while everyone has tried to comprehend its hidden meaning. Science tries to put everything into relationships, numbers, percentages, theories, laws, observations, frames of reference, and physical manifestations like temperatures, pressures, conditions in the past, present and make hypothetical predictions. The universe in return is cold and seems not to care if we have been observing it or not. We consider the what, where, why, when and how. We are the only ones that seem to have any type of reason to explain time. Time, because of our mortality, has a perceived negative value in that we as humans come into existence only to quickly burn up and pass away never to return again.

Time exists for me as an unknown, like existence itself to play itself out as it will. I'm glad I have this opportunity to witness all that has been put before me as a self-reflective being. The connections we forge while we live are of major importance. Family, friends and the trip along the way make the time we have here the only thing we have for sure.

Mastering Business (Continued)

I was having fun, but as the academic year progressed, the pressure was beginning to mount. First semester exams, in particular, was where it began to ramp up. More to the point, the exam for Foundations for Management Thought was the tough one. It had an incredibly high failure rate, which for international students was not good news; if you failed it, your visa was cancelled. So there was not only pressure just to pass the unit, but your entire university course and the life you indented to build on the back of it was in jeopardy. When I think about it, that's a huge consequence for one exam.

But I had a plan for this particular exam. I have a photographic memory. When I was young studying Hindi in high school, I would memorize the text book. I couldn't speak the language that well, but I could recall the rules as they were written in the book. I was going to do a similar thing for Foundations with the source material, a book written by the lecturer.

Of the eight philosophers covered in the course, the exam would be on four of them. I took a gamble. I studied only six and skipped two. If they were the two that happened to be on the exam, I could easily fail. But I was quietly confident based on the way I'd observed the professor's tone in class. I felt I had a good idea of what was going to pop up in the exam.

I developed a superstition around this time too. I'd taken to playing keepy-uppies with a soccer ball, which involves juggling the ball using only the feet, knees, chest and head to keep the ball from hitting the ground. I would count how many times I bounced the ball off my feet. I concentrated on a class, and however many times I juggled the ball, that would be my score. So instead of studying, I spent my time with the soccer ball!

A lot of my friends, perhaps rightly, were concerned that I was setting myself up to fail. They thought I wasn't studying hard enough. But I felt I was okay.

At the end of first semester, exams were held across four days, Monday to Thursday. It was very intense doing an MBA in a year. Foundations was my third exam. A bunch of us met in a car park beforehand and had three shots of tequila each. Everyone needed to calm themselves, so this was how we did it. Though, to be honest, I wasn't nervous.

We went into the exam building, shuffled in silently and expectantly. I sat at a table at random and inspected the paper. And wouldn't you know it, the philosophers I'd studied were all on the exam. So I simply did a brain dump of everything in my memory relating to each of the four subjects. I was the first to finish, I got up and walked out.

Out of the 30 who sat for the exam, 10 failed. I managed to sail through with an 80. And you know what, my keepy-uppie superstition was right: I'd done exactly 80!

The Future Comes to Me

Following term one, a lady from Career Advice asked me to come to her office. She told me that they offer an internship program to the top performing students in each term. They wanted to offer it to me. There was an opportunity in an area called sustainability with an American-listed IT company. The university wanted to know if I was interested.

I politely declined. Firstly, I didn't have the faintest idea about sustainability, and I'd never really thought about climate change. I didn't know what it actually meant, and I certainly didn't really want to do any work. At that point, I just wanted to have fun. I said, "Thanks, but no thanks. I'm thinking of going into a career in strategic finance or marketing." I wanted to let her down gently, so I gave her a little white lie.

But the Career Advice lady was persistent, bless her. A couple of days later she came back to me saying, "Kaushik, have you put any thought into that conversation we had?" I thought I'd rejected it! She told me it was a great company and an interesting topic. I was still none the wiser about sustainability. I didn't want to go around planting trees. I tried to put her off again, but she wasn't having it. She told me they had a week to fill the place, and she asked that I at least go to a meeting at their head office to meet the vice-president of marketing at the time—and later on, my mentor—and the vice president of operations. Which is to say, I was more or less steamrolled into it.

I went along with it. What's the worst that could happen? Three of us from the university went along to that meeting: myself, the Career Advice lady and an academic who would become my PhD supervisor later on. It was my first corporate meeting; I'd never been involved in one before. I'd tried to look good; I'd bought a suit, but it didn't sit well on me. No doubt it looked like my first corporate meeting as well!

Of course, I hadn't done a lot of research on the company—and by "not a lot" I mean zero—but I was quickly brought up to speed. I learned about their vision for and definition of sustainability. I didn't say anything, a silent observer as always.

Then they asked me, "What's your ambition? What do you want to do? What's your thing?" In true Kaushik fashion, I was able to cobble together a quick roundup of my CV and, in that moment, managed to tailor it to a sustainability framework. Whether they saw through it or not, I don't know. But they must have seen something in me. I think, in the end, something clicked, they'd found someone who was slightly eccentric, a little bit exotic, and had a very strategic toolkit.

Now, while I didn't fully understand this space, I did understand the value proposition of turning anything into a commercial proposition. And I told them as much, and I think they connected with that. Also, little did I realize at the time, they wanted an intern to come in and roll out some projects that would save them a ton of money. That was basically what the internship was.

Normally, when people get into the sustainability space, they do so out of passion. That wasn't the case for me. I saw the early signs of a way to make something of myself; not necessarily for saving the planet, but more for carving out a future for myself.

In an MBA, you'll hear a lot of jargon, talk of frameworks and career pathways. No-one had ever talked to me about corporate social responsibility (CSR), sustainability, saving the planet, human rights, anything like that. I thought they were just basic things you did. You looked after your environment, you looked after people. I never saw that as a career; I just saw that as a basic principle of humanity.

Anyway, we left that meeting and I put it all out of my mind, didn't really give it another thought. In true Kaushik style, I let it go. As soon as we left the room my mind switched off and went into something else.

But soon Career Advice lady was back: "They want you to be their intern for the next six months." And that wasn't all: "One of the outputs from this internship won't be just what you do for the company, but for Macquarie you'll have to write a 20,000-word report and that counts for two units." While writing up such a huge report sounded like hard work, it was a way to dodge two classes in one go. If there was an overriding reason for why I accepted the internship, it was so that I could consolidate a couple of classes.

Needless to say, it was an unexpected turn of events. I hadn't said yes to it yet, and to be honest I was hesitating. But there was a flicker of excitement about it, for once again it was something that had come out of the blue. All I needed to do was harness the Power of Positivity!

Lesson 8: The Power of Positivity

Most people want guarantees because they fear the unknown. Some view going down an unexpected or different life or career path as failure. They assert that their fate is predetermined and that they can do little to change their unfortunate circumstances.

Change requires courage; not everyone is capable of taking this leap of faith. Changing your career, in particular, requires an optimistic attitude. Results require patience, and, along the way, you may doubt yourself and your decisions. This is normal.

However, by adopting a "woe-is-me" attitude, many people remain at jobs or in relationships that make them unhappy. Their self-doubt and fear prevail over their good intentions. But failures and errors are lessons learned. The biggest mistake a person can make is being afraid of making one.

Has there ever been a time when you didn't take a chance because you were afraid you would fail? Perhaps you didn't apply for a job because you didn't think you were qualified, or maybe you were scared to quit smoking because you thought it would be too difficult. A simple shift in attitude, or learning to look at a situation with fresh eyes, can make all the difference.

Expect good and bad surprises. No one ever wants bad news, but your choice lies in how you cope with it. For example, being diagnosed with a serious illness can force you to adopt a new perspective to life. Faith and a positive attitude are essential in accepting a difficult new reality. Those who lose a limb in battle or due to illness or accidents have to decide how to deal with this devastating life change. However painful the adjustment is, many people who suffer misfortunes go on to live wonderful, productive lives. Their circumstances do not determine their happiness.

Attitude and a positive belief system greatly influence whether you enjoy life along the way.

Living life in the moment means "not putting your happiness on hold". Living in the present enables you to be your best self, personally and professionally. People who work in goal-oriented settings may find it hard to enjoy the daily processes of life. The danger lies in becoming so focussed on the destination that you miss the scenery along the journey.

Be inspired by the stories of people who faced adversity and triumphed because of their attitude. Many of these individuals credit faith, loving relationships and a positive outlook for their ability to move forward. They appreciate what they have and don't dwell on what they lack.

Embracing Change

I decided to take the plunge. In true Kaushik style, I'd work it out as I went along. The internship was straightforward. I'd go into the head office twice a week. My project was building a business case for implementing energy-efficient initiatives, such as installing LED light bulbs, basic stuff like that. It might seem underwhelming now, but at the time it was quite ground-breaking. And it was satisfying being able to tell the company that if they invested in this technology, their return on investment would be X and payback would be Y. I told them that they would get their money back in three years or less.

I investigated all areas of the business. I went into their data centres to put forward propositions on how to make the layout better, more efficient, so that it functioned in a way that consumed less energy, required less air-conditioning, etc.

At that stage, I didn't know anything about sustainability. But from the first day I started building good relationships with people. They gave me a lot of information without my even asking for it, information that would help my business case and my internship.

My time was spent doing my analysis, looking at spreadsheets, looking at electricity consumption, looking at figures, talking to LED companies and other tech companies. At the end of the day, I put forward a business case for the organization that would save them a bucket load in energy, a bucket load of cash and reduce their carbon emissions.

Not only did I have to put together a report, I also had to present it to their leadership team. Now, here I was, little old Kaushik, presenting to their Asia-Pacific leadership team about sustainability (and I still wasn't clear on what that word even meant). I knew the dollars, I knew carbon.

In that presentation, I put forward a business case and it got signed off. It was one of the first sustainability business cases in APAC. Not only that, I also had to build a tool for them to measure their carbon emissions going forward, from their air travel, electricity, the data centres, the fleet–everything had to be included.

Honestly, I thought what I was doing was a little bit easy. I understood the numbers and reports; to me it was common sense. The thing that really interested me was the dynamic between myself and my mentors, the vice-presidents I'd met with earlier. I'd never had a mentor before. They cared about me, they showed an interest in me. That went for the wider company too; I worked closely with about 10 people, and they all really looked after me. Throughout the internship, people accepted me with wide open arms, there was no judgement; they respected my background, even though I had very little knowledge on sustainability, they gave me a chance. That was a wonderful feeling. And it helped me to produce better work.

Also, they allowed me to talk, allowed me to express my views. They listened and backed me up and taught me to present a business case. I also enjoyed the feeling of going into an office. I'd never formally done that. I'd always been on a tennis court, so it was very cool. Growing up, I saw my dad doing that, and now I was going into an office dressed in suits and ties and taking meetings and hearing all the lingo that I didn't really understand but sounded important. It was just so different to Macquarie. I think I needed both, the corporate and the academic. I had my friends. I had that immature side I could go back to. I needed the balance, the social and the professional. I still need it to this day, everybody does.

My time with the IT company was about figuring out a potential niche where I could have an impact and develop a career. Nevertheless, I was still unsure about my future. I still didn't know where I was headed. I didn't have a plan. These sorts of things don't come to me. While they seem logical to the majority, the question of the future doesn't bother me. There are so many life decisions that I just don't think about. I'm more about the immediate: What's the plan for tonight? What's the plan for tomorrow? How do I have fun? Over the years I have learned the importance of not worrying too much about the future and Enjoying the Moment.

Lesson 9: Enjoy the Moment

Many people lose the ability to laugh when things get tough. People who make a habit of laughing are more resourceful, dynamic and resilient. Something as simple as being stuck in traffic can make you feel helpless and frustrated. The next time you are in bumper-to-bumper traffic, instead of cursing under your breath, tell a joke to your passengers. Laughter will make you feel better, both physically and mentally.

Consider your recent reaction to a stressful situation. Would humour or a shift in attitude have alleviated your stress? Find enjoyment in your daily routine. From the moment you get out of bed, set your intentions for the day. Make a deliberate effort to embrace the morning and whatever it brings. Few people put "enjoy myself" on their list of short or long-term goals, because they are overly focussed on outcomes instead of process. As a result, people put their happiness on hold. They believe they'll be happy only, for instance, when they can buy their dream home or when they get a promotion.

Caption: Sunset at Silveron, NSW

Lesson 10: Prioritize Happiness

Focussing on what you don't have creates a barrier to happiness. Many people struggle with "living in the moment", remaining so single-mindedly intent on their goals that they miss the joy in life's simple pleasures. Society promotes the belief that you need material things to be happy. Although nice possessions enhance your life, they can't provide the same fulfilment as a good relationship with a loved one or with yourself. Many experts now believe that you can learn to be happy. Through classes, seminars, books and online forums, you can tap into the secrets of people who have studied happiness and achieved it.

Make happiness "your number one priority". Change things that upset your "natural state" of gladness. For instance, a difficult co-worker, a sick parent or natural disasters are all outside factors that can undermine your contentment. In the face of a challenge, laugh or think of something that brings joy, such as your good health or your life partner. Focusing on the negative will only make you more miserable.

When movie star Christopher Reeve became paralyzed during an equestrian competition in 1995, he decided not to let his medical condition determine his happiness or worth. You can conquer a negative thought pattern by embracing happiness. Every day is a new opportunity to begin a constructive routine. Exercises that foster positivity include articulating gratitude, stating affirmations, visualizing positive outcomes, and engaging in physical activity. Expressing kindness toward others instantly boosts your spirits, so pay someone a compliment or treat a friend to a cup of coffee.

Life Will Always Throw Curveballs

Without my realizing it, the internship was pivotal for me. I managed to land a job out of it, and I ended up being of considerable value to the company. They paid me for my work and gave me excellent reference letters. I was still getting used to collecting recommendation letters. That's something I've learned to do really well. I'm good at getting feedback quickly and I document it, collect it and then release it when I need to.

That was the start of my sustainability career. I converted that internship into a 20,000-word report for Macquarie, which would go one to be the foundation of my PhD. Although I didn't realize it at the time, that internship was actually the platform that was going to take me somewhere I'd never considered. And that report, which I mainly wrote for a shortcut, ended up paving the way for me to becoming a Doctor.

Following my internship, I pretty much sailed through the rest of that year. My grades were solid; I was going to pass easily. I was also in the midst of my first long-term romantic relationship. Long-term for me, at least. It was with an Asian girl who I'd met early in the year and we'd started going out around April. It lasted all year, until the time came for us to pack up in December. My mum came to help me move back to India, which I had to do until I started my PhD in June of the following year (not that I knew I would be doing a PhD at that stage, because of course I hadn't planned it!). My girlfriend and I decided to try to make the long-distance relationship work while she was back home in Korea and I was in India.

So it was back home to live with my parents. Once again, I had no plan, no direction. I was lost. And now I had a girlfriend in another country. I was also starting to realize that I wasn't that young anymore. I couldn't just keep floundering. I'd never done a long-distance relationship before. We loved each other and wanted to try and make it work. There were lots of unknowns.

At this time my dad was now semi-retired but still consulting with the company he'd run in Nigeria. He was, however, also trying to start his own business. He suggested I run the business with him. We needed to get contacts and clients in China. I had no other prospects, so I took it on. I was also thinking about how to get to my girlfriend in Korea.

I was trying to hatch a little plan; if I could use some of these contacts, maybe I could get myself near Korea. I found a supplier in Yiwu in China, which was promising. Then I found a chemical supplier who made electronics; they also made chemicals in South Korea. I asked my girlfriend to visit them at their head office, to get contact details. Despite my ulterior motive, I was actually well on the way to formalizing a proper business structure for my dad's venture.

I put it to my parents that I should be based in China, that I could work in Yiwu, and I spoke to my girlfriend about making things work between there and Seoul. My parents, unfortunately, were not very receptive. They were more interested in getting me to Nigeria so that I could receive the goods and sell them on. But my mind was more on the girl, not the business.

Things got messy. My heart wasn't in the business. It caused lots of problems between myself and my parents. We had lots of arguments during that time, very heated ones. It was actually quite traumatic. There were times when I'd storm out of the house, threatening to leave for good.

But then, during all the turmoil, I received an email from a lecturer who'd been on the committee for seeing me through the IT company internship. He was just checking in on me, but he also happened to mention the possibility of doing a PhD in sustainability on the back of the internship. Now, as you've probably guessed by now, I'd always hated studying. I didn't even want to do a Bachelor's degree, let alone an MBA and then a PhD. It was just not on my radar at all. But now here was an idea that could get me out of India, out of this nightmare situation with my parents, and back to Australia. That made the decision for me. The problem, though, was twofold: On one hand, there was my parents who would undoubtedly roll their eyes and say, "You want to do what?! Why don't you just get a job and get married to a nice Indian Hindu girl?" That's what they wanted for me. So I had to convince them of my passion for the project (at which I did a good job of pretending). There was also the additional problem of cost. To do a PhD at that time was $102,000, and my parents didn't have that kind of money to throw around. So I made them a deal. If they paid for the first semester, I'd somehow find a way to get a scholarship. Eventually, they assented.

Normally, the way to do a PhD is that you identify your supervisor and you come up with a research proposal. This was not the way I came to it. My supervisor approached me, for starters. And, little did I know, I already had the proposal more or less done in the form of the 20,000-word report. Without that, I couldn't have gotten in.

I think my supervisor knew that I had that report in hand. He probably felt that he needed a doctoral student, because he could be quite difficult and I don't think many people wanted to work with him. With me, he saw a baked-in PhD. So, without really realizing what my supervisor was going to be like, I just went with it.

Dr. Kaushik

And so, I packed my bags again and returned to Sydney. On PhD orientation day, I met a guy who was doing a biography on Rupert Murdoch's grandfather. We would become very good friends. My MBA network had broken apart at the end of the course; most of my friends were from other countries and they'd all returned home. Via some sweet talking to the accommodation administrator at the Macquarie University Village, I was able to get bumped up the waiting list and, eventually, into some nice digs. That was a good start to my chapter two in Sydney.

All this time, I was having weekly chats with my girlfriend, the frequency of which were reducing. Things were starting to cool in that sphere. She wasn't coming back to Sydney. There was no future for us, but neither of us wanted to do anything about it.

As for my PhD project itself, there was no real plan, and the plan we did have was quite loose. My supervisor just left me on my own with it.

For that first semester, I was still fee-paying. I was not on a scholarship. One day, I was sitting in my room. And I just decided to visit the scholarship website. Up until then, I'd done no research on how to get a scholarship. And if my dad was not going to fund me beyond the first semester, I needed the scholarship by December.

I noticed that Macquarie University had something called a Macquarie scholarship. There was also something called an Endeavour Scholarship. That was a tough one to get. The Macquarie one was easier, but you didn't get as much money. In any case, I needed one and it didn't matter which because both covered tuition fees and provided a stipend.

For the Endeavour, you needed to have published at least two articles in peer-reviewed journals. At that point, I had little understanding of the path to having an article published. I had no clue how long it takes you to write something; then you have to send it to an editor of a journal. They need about three months to review it and then come back to you for the first set of corrections. The whole process can take six months to a year; sometimes it can take two years, depending on the journal. At first, it seemed like a dead-end. But I'm always searching for angles, ways to work around things and make them work. Just out of curiosity, I thought I'd just look back through pieces I'd written during my MBA.

I'd written some good papers, which had received good grades. It's worth noting at this point that my supervisor was very clear from the outset: I wasn't to publish a paper by myself; it had to be co-authored because my supervisor needed his name on it. That's just how it works. I knew this, but I also knew I was on a tight schedule. If I was going to make the publication thing work, I was going to have to act fast in an environment where the wheels turned very, very slowly.

I found the papers I thought were my best. One was on carbon tax and the other was a marketing essay. Then I set about finding the right journals. The key was to not aim too high. I searched for smaller journals put out by small universities. If figured that most people would be aiming high with their academic papers, trying for the big names. But I wasn't too concerned about that; I just needed to have mine published, it almost didn't matter where. If a smaller journal accepted my work, I believed I could push them along a bit to get everything turned around in time.

I found some journals that fit my criteria, got my papers in order, gave them a quick spit and polish, and made my submissions. I immediately followed up with an email to the editors introducing myself and politely asking for their feedback as soon as possible.

I'm a very persistent person. Every three or four days, I would hound them. And it worked; within a month I received some feedback. I needed to make some corrections and get them back to the editors. Within a day, I turned around the corrections and sent them off. Then I just kept pushing. Within a week or two I got the acceptance emails for two papers. The beauty of this was that I had also recently learned from the Scholarships Committee that the publications listed in my application didn't have to be in print at the time of application; they just had to have been accepted. I just needed an email acceptance of the papers. Luckily, I was also able to befriend one of the people in the scholarship team at Macquarie. They knew that I needed the publications, and went out of their way to help me with my application to make it as strong as possible. It was bizarre, having all these people working for me.

Things were looking good. I'd gotten my publications, I reached out to a few former mentors and teachers for letters of recommendation, packaged it up, put a bow on it, and submitted it to the Macquarie Scholarships Committee. Then I went to my contact there and asked them to speed up the steering committee process, which they did. And so within a bit over two months, from looking up the scholarships online to final approval, I got a letter saying, "Dear Kaushik, you have been granted an Endeavour Scholarship." I'd done it. I couldn't believe it.

And that was not all. One of the students who received the Endeavour Scholarship the previous semester had pulled out. So the committee had an extra $13,000 and had to give it to someone or else they risked their level of funding being decreased the following year. So they said they'd backdate my application and give it to me. Lo and behold, it was exactly the amount my father had paid for my first semester tuition fees, and so I was able to pay him back straightaway; he wasn't out of pocket one penny.

Learning to Diversify

But while I landed on my feet in terms of the scholarship, I didn't feel so lucky when it came to my supervisor. He was particularly hard on me. As I said, he had a reputation for being difficult to work with. He was very blunt when critiquing my work, saying things like, "What sort of writing is this? Don't you have a plan? Are you wasting people's time?" I was trying to find my way with the project, and hearing that while you're already uncertain about your direction just was not helpful at all. If he'd brought me in because he needed to supervise a PhD candidate, he was not doing himself any favours. I'd leave our meetings more confused than when I went in. He'd had students before who'd withdrawn from projects or sought out other supervisors. So I knew who I was up against.

But I stayed on the bull. I listened, I took the criticism, I observed. Even today my mum says, "It's a miracle you graduated through him." To be honest, he was a bit of a bully. One of the good things to come out of those initial conversations was that we agreed to do a thesis by publication. There were two ways to do a PhD: You could publish your research as a book, or you could publish papers, say seven papers, one for each chapter.

But again, I saw an opportunity. Or perhaps, a shortcut. I didn't need to write this hulking great study. I could just write short, sharp papers and publish them, and get the whole thing over with. What's more, if it was already a collection of published papers by the time it got to my examiners, they would likely see it as peer-reviewed work and be less harsh with their criticism.

It was around this time, that I met with a person who'd been my Human Resources lecturer during my MBA. I'd formed a good bond with him; he would go on to be instrumental in my career going forward. Additionally, his wife worked for a large consultancy. For my thesis, I wanted to interview companies and collect data that would inform my hypothesis.

We spoke about getting the company his wife worked for involved, to which he was very responsive. We also spoke about jobs, and he told me that he was looking for a research assistant to help with his own PhD, which was looking into HR practices in law firms. It was a great opportunity. I had the scholarship, but I needed the extra work.

So, instantly I got a 20-hour-a-week contract. I was very efficient in delivering the work. I would take about six hours to do 20 hours' work. Of course, I'd still get paid for twenty hours. It was all about efficiency, developing my own methods to get things done. But it was also a question of living how I wanted to live, working how I wanted to work, and often ignoring typical definitions of productivity.

Lesson 11: On Being Productive

I used to think productivity was about doing more in less time, so I would do more. I had it all wrong. We live in a culture of *more*. We need to earn more, buy more, say more, do more or get more. When I took my first job out of college, I worked long hours for about two years. At the time I wasn't married and I didn't have kids so this was my top priority. All I wanted to do was learn and get better. But I knew it wasn't sustainable. I had to figure out how to be "more productive".

I had a murky thought in 2013: What if productivity starts with doing less? This question feels strange because productivity is measured by output over input. In other words, if I can do more in an hour today than I did yesterday, I am considered more productive. This is a simple "do more" mindset. It ignores a couple of critical points. When I measure productivity, I look at whether I produced meaningful things well.

Focus on the Right Things

For the longest time, I would focus on things that were immediate. If it was screaming for attention, I would add it to my list and get to work. I was so focused on doing, that I never stopped to think about what needed to be done.

It starts with clear goals, either personal or professional. If I'm not working on the things that matter the most, I'm working on the wrong things.

Most people believe that all the tasks on their list are important. That may be true, but they are not all equal. Prioritization matters. Often times I would knock out lower priority work because it was easy and I could get it done quicker. This was another big mistake.

My mindset now is very different. I have a list ranked by importance and I focus on doing the most important things well.

Motivation plays another important role in my definition of productivity. Figuring out what I value and why, helps me make the right choices with my personal and professional time.

Speaking of time, the easiest, and often hardest, way to find more is to say no. Have you heard of this line: "There was not enough time in the day"? I've always heard this line and I'd repeat it myself. But this way of thinking can send us down the wrong path. What people are saying is there's no time left to do the things that matter. This is a prioritization problem, not a "do more" problem. After I sort out my time, it's easier to see the things that have to drop.

Create

It's easy to confuse busy work with real work. I have bad news: answering emails, sitting in meetings and knocking off tasks that are low in importance is not real work. The biggest problem I've seen is that busy work gets done before real work. It seems to always take centre stage because that work is immediate. Creating something is harder, so it gets pushed to the bottom of the list.

We get lost when we focus on activity vs. impact. I've had many different roles in my career and I've always had the most impact when I created something. This might be a product spec, a marketing message, a strategy or a sales pitch. Of course, what gets created needs to align with what matters to the company.

Do It Well

There is so much focus on efficiency that it often leads to poor work. If I was working on the right things and I did a sloppy job, it would be a complete waste of time. It wouldn't matter that I was working on the right thing. It wouldn't matter that I created something. If it isn't done well, not only will I not have a positive impact, I may have a negative one.

Once I'm clear on what work matters, then I turn to creating. Once I start that process, I can look for ways to be more efficient, but never at the expense of quality. Of course quality is subjective. There is always a point where it's better to call it done than keep working it until it's perfect. Every situation is different. Figuring this one out often comes down to experience.

I can attribute a lot of my success and even happiness to my "productivity". When I was working hard on low-value tasks I would feel stressed and underpaid. In reality, I was underachieving and sacrificing my health in the process. The more I was able to create things that mattered, the more success I saw.

Create Time

We all get the same amount of time each day. What differs and sets people apart is how they choose to spend it. Make no mistake, we are "spending" time. Which begs the question, what is our time worth? When I was young, I didn't think my time was worth much. I made minimum wage like a lot of others. After going to college, I got a raise. The world told me my time was worth three times what I used to make.

The biggest problem I see with this thinking is the hourly part. It focuses on short term output. Compare this to an investment. This is long-term output. The more I think about my time as an investment, the better decisions I seem to make with how to apply it.

After I figured out that this process was helping me be more successful, I wanted to do more of it. That meant I needed to create time. Since I can't create a 25-hour day, I had to cut out the things I was doing that wasted time.

I looked at my day and found a lot of opportunities. I cut out reading news and staying up late. I also decided to get up earlier. Combined, I created 20 hours a week to focus on the most important work I can. To help make sure I don't lose time, I try to stay healthy. I eat well, exercise and get a good night's sleep.

Be a Doer

> *"The way to get started is to quit talking and begin doing"*

– Walt Disney

At some point it's time to get down to work. There is no substitute for getting started. If I don't have everything mapped out, I will start with the first obvious step. My goal is to keep moving forward.

There have been plenty of times when I failed to take action. Sometimes it's hard to get started. But a little action goes a long way. It creates momentum and helps me move on to each following piece of work. A lot of people think this is hard. In fact, a few of my friends tell me I'm the most productive person they know.

Here's the thing: I'm not special. It does take discipline to make these decisions, but these decisions are not hard. Anyone can do what I've done and even do a better job. I do it because productivity is important to me. It's important that I work on things that matter. I love to create, and I get a lot of satisfaction from it. Since my name is on the work, I always want it to be something that I can be proud of. It's taken me a long time to figure this out. Now that I have, I can tell you that I am living a happier, healthier and more fulfilling life. In the words of Margaret Bonnano: "Being rich is having money; being wealthy is having time."

Getting My Doctorate

I was very busy. But I wasn't, and never have been, "too busy". I hate saying I'm busy. I hate that word. It's about being efficient, effective, and productive. That was and is my motto. And it has worked well.

At that time, I was in a routine. I've found that the best way to remain productive. I'd wake up at 9 a.m. and go to a coffee shop. I became best friends with the baristas and regulars there. That's how much time I spent there. And I spent a fortune! So, in one coffee shop next to where I lived, I'd have an avocado, egg, and bread, and coffee. Or if I walked all the way to work, I'd have a big breakfast and an iced coffee. Needless to say, I started gaining weight. After breakfast, I'd mosey on down to my research office. I'd get there at 10:30 a.m. There was a Jewish woman in her 90s who was doing her PhD. She'd come in around 11 a.m. and sit behind me. We'd chitchat until she ran out of energy. And then, I'd do a bit of work. Again, efficient, effective, and productive. I had a schedule and I followed that to a tee, which meant I'd be done by 1 p.m. I focussed my energies on putting in two hours of work writing up my thesis each day. It doesn't sound like much, but as the weeks and months ticked by, it all started to add up.

Then it was time for socializing. I walked over to the Macquarie Shopping Centre by about 2 p.m. where they had an ice-skating rink, Hoyts Cinemas, and food courts. So, I'd meet a different friend there each day and just hang out for the rest of the afternoon. That was my routine. For two and a half years, that's how my days were structured. And it enabled me to finish my thesis in that time, even though my scholarship gave me four years.

That's the benefit of having a plan and a structure. Too many people like to complicate things. If you've got a plan and you stick to it, you'll get things done. I got my PhD in two and a half years by sticking to my plan. I was focussed when I needed to be, which meant that I could spend a lot of time socializing, being with the people I wanted to be with. That's important. But it was also important that I was creating, I was putting a bit of myself into my thesis each and every day. Later on, this daily effort would expand into many areas and cross many disciplines. Basically, it's a way of having many fingers in many pies, and I found that the more I put out there, the more things came to me, often out of the blue!

Lesson 12: Create More Than You Consume

A big part of putting yourself out there is to create. Write, Tweet, take photos, draw, launch a podcast, a newsletter, a local event, an online community. The idea of creating more than you consume is a close relative of the classic maxim "Give more than you take". If you give your time and share your ideas, people will find you. And even if they don't, thanks to the generation effect, you will learn much more in the process than if you limited yourself to passive consumption.

The Dot

I still had hurdles to clear. It was during the early months of my PhD that I received one of the best pieces of advice I've received in my life. It is something I still carry with me and swear by to this day. And, of all people, it was my supervisor who gave it to me, despite our somewhat difficult relationship. So I have him to thank for this.

Not only did I have to formulate a plan for my thesis, I also had to come up with an interesting, engaging title for it. Something that would make people want to read it, but also explain clearly what the thesis was about. I had a title in mind, which was very long, but comprehensive, something like 25 words long (not unheard of in academic circles). Still, it was a bit epic. I submitted that to my supervisor and almost immediately he sent a reply email with a single line (the one you always dread from a superior!): "See me in my office."

Next day, I went into his office feeling pretty damn nervous. He told me to take a seat and I quickly, obediently sat. There was a moment of silence and I was wondering what the hell he wanted to see me about. I could tell by the atmosphere of the room that it wasn't going to be anything good. Was he going to kick me off the program? Had he heard me complaining about him? He certainly had an ego problem, so it wasn't out of the realm of possibility that he'd be offended and want retribution.

"So, is this your topic? Is this your title?" he said. I nodded. And then he said, "Are you trying to change the world?" I nodded, not because I wanted to charge out there and change everything, mind you, but more because I wanted to have some sort of positive impact. I couldn't think of how else to respond.

My supervisor pointed to the folder on my lap. "Give me that white piece of paper and a pencil," he said. I clipped open my folder, removed a sheet of paper and handed it to him along with my pencil. He proceeded to draw a circle in the middle of the page.

"The white space inside the circle is the depth and breadth of knowledge that exists in the universe," he said indicating the area he was referring to. Then he placed a little dot inside the big circle and said, "That's you, right there. This tiny speck. That's the impact your PhD is going to have. It's probably the impact your whole life's going to have. You need to be happy with that, Kaushik, and stop trying to change the world by being the entire circle."

It was certainly a big reality check for me. A wake-up call. It almost just derailed me completely. It was full on. I couldn't digest what had just happened and the way that it was delivered to me. But to this day, that's the one piece of feedback that has had the biggest impact on me. Of all the things that had been said to me by teachers and coaches and bullies and parents, this line about the dot is what has stuck. Focussing on the dot has helped me to sleep better at night. It has helped me realize that I don't need to take everything so seriously, that I can't do much about anything.

Of course, there are times and situations where I get a bit overwhelmed by things, for example my dad's health. But other than those sorts of things, I just think about what's my dot, my tiny role in a particular business or a setting or whatever it is. And if I hit that dot, if I do what I can do, I'm happy.

For many others, that dot is not enough. That's what stresses them out, that's where the worry comes in. My dot is a tiny little dot. I have my supervisor to thank for that. And that's what I did, I worried about that miniscule mark on the sprawling white page. My 25-word thesis title was pared down to about 10. I submitted my proposal, presented it, and received really good reviews.

Applying a Skillset Across Different Fields

I was fortunate that I structured my thesis the way I did. There were two options: first was to do a deep dive into a single company from a sustainability perspective; the second, was to do case studies of a number of different companies from all over the world. I decided on the latter, and I'm glad I did, because it put me in touch with so many people and would go on to open up all sorts of opportunities.

I spoke to just about every company I could think of, from all sorts of industries. Companies such as one of the biggest banks in Canada, a biotech company in Australia, and two automobile manufacturers in Europe. I spent a long time sending emails and phoning people. Many were quite hesitant because no doubt they received lots of requests to participate in research. I was a fresh-eyed kid, eager and enthusiastic to get my project done.

I was basically selling my research. To be honest, it wasn't groundbreaking, but I sold it like it was. I think what appealed to these companies was that I sold it in a way that wasn't complicated; too many academics overcomplicate their proposals. Academics are often quite linear in their approach and they're not really open to change. They've got a certain style, a certain way of thinking, whereas corporates are probably a little bit more practical, pragmatic, and hopefully a little bit more open-minded. Often the two don't mix. But I found a good way to bridge the divide.

I always spoke corporate, even though I was still quite academic, and it's thanks to observing my dad and all the tennis coaching. I haven't always been part of the academic world; by this time in my life I also had a bit of real-world experience. I was doing an academic project, but I had a way of not allowing idealism to run away with the show. I could be sensitive to the mindsets of the businesspeople I was talking to. I could see both sides.

It's something I'm conscious of even today. In my current corporate role, whenever I go to a site I'm bridging the divide between head office and the mine workers. They are two very different worlds, despite being the same company. I am able to gel with them in a way that makes it agreeable for both sides, so each can get their point of view across. Being able to speak both languages, if you like, makes it much easier to keep everyone happy.

A case in point is when, in one of my previous roles, I was sent to Colombo, Sri Lanka, to conduct an audit at a telecommunications firm. I was coming in from the Melbourne office, so obviously I was an outsider, and therefore it was imperative for me to establish trust between myself and the people for whom the audit was intended. I'd never worked in telecommunications before, and they knew that, which meant I had to convince them that I knew what I was talking about, and that our interests were aligned. They didn't want somebody coming in shooting from the hip with half-baked ideas. It would have been relatively easy for them to think, "Who is this young guy sitting in his Melbourne office coming over here and telling us how to run a telecom business in Sri Lanka?" In a way, I had to wing it, because it was a new industry for me. But, still, I knew the basic principles of running this type of business, and I drew a lot on my skills in other areas to convince them of this.

I was coming from a place in which I was also there to learn, and I've found that that puts people more at ease. I don't take the position that I'm an expert who thinks he knows everything. I try to leave my ego at the door and make them feel I'm on their side. Which, at the end of the day, I am.

Eventually, we all got along largely thanks to my approach. It's about finding the right vocabulary, having patience and a willingness to listen. At the end of that day, we provided our findings to the general manager. I was straight with him, and in the debrief session with the leadership team I pointed out all these gaps in their business, areas in which they could improve massively. And they must have listened because my findings were a catalyst for some major changes in that company.

At the end of the day, people are simply afraid of not being heard or understood. I'm always careful to ensure the other party is heard, and know that they're being heard. So after I've put forward both sides, as I see them, then I open it up for a calm, reasonable discussion.

Whereas other auditors, whenever I've listened to them, certainly do not talk like that. They provide their recommendation, listen briefly to what the other person had to say, then want to argue about it. I try to keep it all smooth. It's not productive when things get heated.

Later on, after my PhD research had come out, many companies told me how much they appreciated my approach, how I was able to meet them halfway, or even simply go over to their side completely.

I was very sensitive to their needs, and I could tailor a proposal to highlight the ways in which what I was doing would be of use to them. I knew they would find it valuable, and so I had to show them where the value lay. Sometimes I might have been a bit manipulative, but that was just to get them across the line. It was for their own good!

I remember being on the phone with the director of one of the biggest pharmaceutical companies in Australia, who at first didn't want to know about me or my research. His tone had "Why are you bothering me?" all over it. But I didn't let go; I just kept going at it. I was persistent. I made a semi-informed guess at where they were on their sustainability journey, and tried to add details that would entice them to get on-board.

Lesson 13: The Importance of Being Patient

Impatience often prevents us from achieving our goals. Patience leaves us calm and relaxed. It helps to reduce stress in otherwise trying situations. In the long run, learning how to be patient in everyday life will only help you down the road. A few tips on improving your patience levels:

Take Note of What Makes You Impatient

World famous martial artist and cultural icon Bruce Lee once said, "Patience is not passive, on the contrary, it is concentrated strength." This quote highlights the role of awareness in practicing patience. Only when we consciously perceive situations in which we become impatient can we actively do something about it and learn how to be more patient.

What Consequences Can Your Impatience Have?

Remember that no matter the situation, impatience won't get you anywhere. In fact, it's much more likely to prevent you from achieving your goals. With a little patience, you can master situations better and in the end you will be calm, balanced and relaxed.

Practice Makes Perfect

Take a moment and think about what parts of your day made you especially happy or what aspects of your life you're particularly grateful for in the particular moment. These moments of mindfulness allow you to consciously recall positive moments—often we only remember negative situations.

How to Deal with Setbacks

We all experience minor setbacks. Some are brought about by events or conditions we have no control over. Therefore, it's always good to mentally plan for delays so you're not caught completely flat-footed when they happen. Whether trying to learn patience or planning a work project: try not to see setbacks as a personal defeat. Instead, think about the positives you can take from them. Setbacks can help you gain valuable experience and insight, which helps you to develop as person and emerge stronger.

Racism

I'm used to observing. I like observing. Which means I'm used to being the outsider. Perhaps I'm too used to it. Growing up as an Indian in Nigeria, then being one of the only brown-skinned people at the tennis academy and all the trouble I had there, had all probably conditioned me to take the outsider perspective. This might explain why I have often overlooked things that can be considered racist. I was talking on a podcast recently, and the Indian host explained how people would often say to her in job interviews, "Oh, your English is so good."

Of course, I've had many, many job interviews in which people have said exactly the same thing, and until it was pointed out to me, I never took that as a racist comment. I never perceived it that way. I just thought, "Okay. Thanks for mentioning that. Whether I'm brown, white, black, yellow, I guess my English is fine." I never thought that it should come as a *surprise* to anyone. But I guess that's how it's meant, even if it is subconsciously.

When I thought about it, I noticed that I have, in fact, experienced racism—quite often. For example, when I went to very posh networking events, there was often a subtle racism. I now tell many of my mentees who are of colour. When I go to these supposedly classy networking events, no one talks to me. I've got a bit of a baby face. But I get the impression people don't take me seriously or think that I have anything to offer.

My wife often says to me, "You've got a PhD. You've got all these accolades. Why don't you show off? Why don't you let people know who they're dealing with?" But I'm a fairly quiet person. I don't tell anyone anything about me. I always try to ask questions and listen. That's just me. I don't like coming across as "better".

I admit, though, I do take pleasure in surprising people. For example, I went to this networking event where there were millionaires, CEOs and vice-presidents. When I arrived, I happened to merge into a group of elderly Caucasian people. I thought I'd join in the conversation, say "hi". This is pretty standard behaviour for these events. You're there to meet people, that's what everyone is doing, so people tend to be less standoffish and usually more inclusive.

Nobody in that group acknowledged me. Nobody even looked at me. I was standing there for ten minutes while they sipped their champagne and spoke about human rights and climate change and things they thought nobody else really understood. So I just stood there. I didn't move. I stood there with a smile. Now, many people would feel threatened in that situation. It's understandable to feel the need to get away, to think it wasn't working or even that it was a bit embarrassing. But it didn't bother me. I just stood there. I was the outsider—a role I have played all my life. I was actually quite comfortable with it.

It became quite clear who the most arrogant person in the group was: a lady standing right next to me. She saw me approach and join the group right next to her at her elbow, but she didn't say a word or even look at me and smile. Nothing. After standing there for a time, the conversation moved on to the topic of PhDs. The woman beside me piped up with, "Oh, yes, I've got a PhD. I did it in eight years!" She was rather eager to let everyone know how amazing she was with her PhD. Well, this was my moment. I knew about PhDs, knew all about them. It was a bit cheeky of me, but I said, "Oh, did you? Eight years? Wow. I did mine in two point five years." Suddenly their attitude towards me was completely different.

I experience that sort of thing often. When I go to conferences, I'll be standing around or sitting in the audience. Nobody will say a word to me, but then they'll see me giving the keynote or speaking. And then suddenly Kaushik becomes important, and suddenly he has a swarm of bees around him.

I do find it all a bit of fun. I don't know if it's all to do with the colour of my skin, but I like disarming people. I thrive on it, in some cases. The element of surprise.

I want to put bullies in their place, and bullying comes in physical and emotional forms.

Throughout my corporate career, I haven't felt targeted racially all that much. Still, I think I get preyed upon more for my demeanour, for the way I am. I look like someone who can easily be targeted, who can easily be squashed, who can easily be bullied, who can easily be made fun of, and that's just the way I come across. Unfortunately; I can't help it.

But that's all superficial stuff. I've got a high tolerance level and can handle a lot; I internalize a lot. But I can also be a bit of a stonefish. You've got to be careful where you tread! Because once a line is crossed, then that's it. It's true, I've lost a lot of friends because of where I drew the line. But you have to. You have to set your own boundaries and guard them, otherwise people will walk all over you. I tend to give people many chances. But if they want to continue bullying me, I'll stand up for myself. I've experienced a shit-load of racism in Australia, much more than in America, that's for sure.

From Student to Teacher

My PhD years rolled on. I'd gotten the scholarship. I'd even gone and gotten myself a girlfriend. Things were gorgeous. My social network was on fire. I got a call from the Career Advice lady, who had basically railroaded me into doing my internship. She had another proposition for me. She said, "Kaushik, I've got a couple of students who need private tutoring for accounting." These were MBA students who needed help with their accounting units. Other than having done one accounting class in my own MBA, I didn't really know anything about the subject. But, of course, I jumped at the chance. I'd wing it and see what happened!

I had to think on my feet, so I used my first student as a bit of a guinea pig. I learnt about management accounting on the job, and winged my way through providing advice on how to pass the exam. I'd done the exam during my own MBA and received a high distinction, so I knew what to expect there.

Regardless of my methods, it worked and she passed the exam with flying colours. Word must have got round, because my one student became two, two became 10, and by the end of my PhD I had up to 40 students. Without meaning to, I'd built my reputation as an accounting tutor.

Part Four

Going Corporate

Finding the Balance: From University to the Workforce

By May 2011, I could see the light at the end of the tunnel. I was wrapping up my thesis and, naturally, I hadn't planned the next step, my next chapter. I would need a job, that's for sure, but I also had another eight months left on my scholarship, so I wasn't going to waste my time doing something I didn't want or need to do. My first thought was all the companies I'd talked to in order to put my thesis together. I'd just start calling around and see what I could get.

So that's what I did; I called them. And they all, without exception, said, "No. You're an international student. We won't sponsor you." That was an unexpected snag. My plan went down the drain within a week.

I wasn't fazed though. I knew something would come my way. Many of the companies I'd called had directed me to a consulting firm. I hadn't bothered calling them because I really wanted to land something with the companies I already knew. But failing that, I called the consulting firm and organized a time to meet with HR.

I met with the director and a senior associate. They asked if I was interested in doing an internship. I told them that I was, but I would eventually need a job and sponsorship. They didn't commit to anything, but I had my scholarship for another few months; I could afford to see how things panned out.

I was talking to one of the largest sustainability consulting firms in Australia. While I did my internship, I didn't look for any other opportunities. I basically put all my eggs in one basket, which is what I do. I continued with my social life, finished off my PhD, commenced a new internship and would see how things went.

Things soon became dicey with regard to my visas. If I had to get a work visa, that meant I had to cancel my student visa, and I didn't want to jeopardize either one. So the timing had to be perfect. I asked the people at my corporate job what they were thinking. Would they keep me on permanently?

The founder of the company was a South Asian based in Melbourne; he flew up to Sydney to meet with me. He basically said, "So what can you offer me? We're a consulting company." Would you believe it, this time I'd done my homework! I was expecting him to ask me this question. Tucked away in my pocket, I had a piece of paper with a list of all my contacts from my PhD. I tried not to sound too smug when I said, "Well, it so happens that I have this piece of paper," and I put it in front of him. He asked me about the kinds of relationships I had with these firms, and I told him the truth: every one of them was solid, and we could surely get a lot of business from the names on that list.

He asked what sorts of things I could offer his company. I basically rattled off the key points of my PhD (without really explaining to him that's what I was doing), informing him of all the sustainability gaps at each company. He smiled, shook my hand and said, "All right. You've got your 457 work visa!" That was the beginning of my career in sustainability.

By that time I'd built quite the resumé. My PhD was just about to be approved, I was tutoring a hell of a lot of students, and I was a "research analyst" (it is usually called a research assistant, but I asked my employer if I could put "analyst" on my resumé and he said, "Put whatever you want.") I'd been an intern at the company my father worked for, I'd been "General Manager" at the tennis academy in Albury, and Environmental Analyst at my first internship. There was a lot in there, and I had learned to leverage my experience.

It's very important to leverage every experience you have. Whenever people look at my LinkedIn, they'll say, "Yours is one of the best LinkedIn profiles we've ever seen." That's because it is always up-to-date, and documents everything about me. If I get a reference letter, it goes on file. Everything I do, goes on there. I had a call centre job at Macquarie University for a while, which was sponsored by one of the world's largest technology companies. For a week, six of us were selected from my cohort to sit in a room with undergrads and other students, and we called alumni to get donations for the Macquarie Graduate School of Management. Afterwards, we got a certificate signed by the CEO of Microsoft, but it read more like a reference letter. It was personalized and gave details of my experience with the company. Even though it was only for a week, no one would know; as far as anyone else was concerned, I had a letter of reference from the CEO of Microsoft.

I was building a toolkit. It's one of my skills. I can make a lot out of nothing. So much of life is about perception. Many people probably didn't even look at that Microsoft reference letter, but I leveraged it and it became one of the key elements in my kit.

Get a Real Job

Researching was now my forte. After a lifetime trying to outrun studies and anything remotely academic, here I was with an MBA and a PhD. After looking like I'd one day be a tennis pro, or even a coach, here I was working in the corporate world, in the area of social responsibility, no less; not in India or Nigeria or the States, but in Sydney, Australia. Things were turning out in entirely unexpected, but not undesirable, ways.

My second internship was an interesting and engaging introduction to the sector. Usually, you would enter one of the big four sustainability consulting firms: KPMG, Ernst & Young, Deloitte, or PricewaterhouseCoopers. But the company I was interning for was starting to disrupt this playing field. Once again, I found myself in the position of the outsider, working in the boutique consulting firm. As I've said before, it's a role I enjoy; it keeps me energized and free to think for myself. Being part of the establishment has never suited me; it comes with too many expectations, too many directives about how you should operate. For me, that's the path to mediocrity.

At the time, my clients ranged from electricity providers and telecommunications companies to industrial conglomerates and airlines. The work was interesting. Mostly, I was looking at identifying issues most material to those companies from environment, social, and governance perspectives. For example, a major electricity and gas retailer was trying to understand what their customers were actually looking for in terms of the company's social responsibilities.

I found that it now suited me because I'd just come from a PhD. We had something called community investments. So, for every dollar invested into the community, I would figure out the return on that investment. I investigated things like greenhouse gas emissions, environmental reporting and auditing for clients, for which I found my first internship instrumental. There, I was exposed to a range of clients in many industries across a range of subject matters from human rights to climate change to strategy to social impact, assurance, to safety.

To be honest, it was a lot to absorb for someone who didn't have much experience in the field. It was really my first gig. But the way that I communicated and the way I came across, and the way I was able to think on my feet made me adapt well into a consulting world.

Soon, however, things started getting political. Most sustainability consulting firms have tools that they use in order to identify gaps in their client's social responsibility strategies. It works like a template that the analyst can lay over the company's operations and show them in black and white where they're strong and where they're not. My job was to identify these gaps and then tell our clients how I could fill those gaps. The trouble was, my current employer didn't have a tool for doing the work; most of the time, we relied on publicly available data and simple discussions with key stakeholders. This was my dot. I couldn't change the whole company; I couldn't change the entire world, but I could do this one thing. I saw the opportunity—a gap in our own processes—to formalize the data-gathering process and make our work more effective and efficient.

So I designed a tool. And it was a pretty good one, too, if I do say so myself. Within ten minutes, a company would be able to see in no uncertain terms where the gaps were and how far along they were on their sustainability journey. But, in my eagerness and naivety, I didn't appreciate that designing something like this is one thing, but integrating it within the company was quite another. You need to take people with you, step by step, and you need to allow things time to go through established channels and procedures for them to be most effective.

Instead of doing these things, and without really thinking too much about it, I sent my design straight to the founder of the company, right to the top. To tell you the truth, I was secretly hoping to impress him.

Which, admittedly, I did. Ordinarily, this would have been a great thing, but I wasn't prepared for the consequences of my hasty actions. The founder of the company sent back excellent feedback, telling me it was just what the company needed, "Let's progress with this!" He was very enthusiastic.

Now, he'd also copied into his reply my boss and her boss. At the time I thought nothing of it, other than being quietly chuffed that I'd made a significant contribution to the company and our operations and that the big boss was happy with me.

It was also at this time that I had my six-month probationary review. One day, not long after I'd received the email from our founder, I was called into a room together with my boss, her boss and the company's HR manager, who had flown up from our headquarters in Melbourne. It all seemed collegial and routine. I was completely oblivious to this being anything other than a performance review. But what followed was an absolute grilling about not going behind people's backs or over their heads. There was a chain of command that needed to be followed. I couldn't just send things on up the line without going through them first. Not only that, but the way in which they told me these things was, as I saw it, unnecessarily aggressive—especially for a HR manager! They questioned my behaviour, my loyalty and the quality of my work.

I turned to stone. I just sat there and just took a beating. I didn't respond, I didn't try to justify myself. I just sat there and absorbed it. By the end of it, I was shattered. Was this what corporate life was? Is this how people were treated? I was stunned. I couldn't believe what I was hearing. I'd heard that big companies treat their graduates well, like gold, because they want to maintain a good reputation, and graduates talk. Well, that's not what I received in that meeting. I copped a verbal beating!

I came out of that meeting and pretty much straightaway called my parents. I told them, "I am on a visa. So, I'm handcuffed to them. I'm stuck." I really was stuck. I couldn't quit, because then I'd have to go back to India, and I very much did not want to do that. And if I were to look for another job, with minimal experience, how marketable was I? I didn't know anything about my brand, my reputation, my experiences. But, the thing about me is, I move on in a day. So, I moved on. I flipped the switch. My focus shifted. I felt that I was ready to move on to another chapter. I just didn't know how to extricate myself from a situation that I knew would only become increasingly toxic.

Come my 12-month review, I called the guy from HR in Melbourne and told him that he would need to come up for it. I wanted him there. Again, it was only the four of us. This time, however, the shoe was on the other foot. We took our seats around a long table in the conference room, the three of them on one side, me on the other. Traditional hierarchies are designed to be intimidating so that those in power might remain in power. But today I wasn't intimidated. I knew what I'd come to say, and I felt I was justified in what I had to tell them. They might not like it, but that was on them; I can't be held responsible for their feelings. I'm responsible only for my own, and as we settled into our places at the table I was keeping my emotions in check, staying focussed on what needed to be said. I wasted no time; in a calm, measured voice, I laid it out for them clearly, firmly but quietly. It's important to stay calm while making a point, lest it become swamped by emotion and muddled thinking. I told them that if they wanted to bully me around because I was beholden to them for a visa, they could forget it. Visa or no visa, I wasn't going to put up with it anymore. I had taken a beating during our last meeting. I was strong enough to take it, and just absorb everything that was being said, even if I didn't agree with a lot of it. I just let it settle, safe in the knowledge that I would address it at a later date.

In business, you're going to have to learn to take a beating from time to time. If you're taking risks and pushing yourself, there *are* going to be times that you fuck it up. Everyone makes mistakes. You've got to learn to deal with the consequences, dust yourself off, learn from your mistakes and get back on it! Learn from it, don't repeat mistakes, but also don't put up with being treated unfairly.

In that conference room that day, I was straight with them, I looked them in the eye. It was all about setting boundaries and sticking to them. Having enough respect for yourself and the people you're working with means putting up boundaries and sticking to them. It's difficult and can be awkward, but you'll feel empowered by going through it. And even if it doesn't pan out exactly as you hope, you'll take courage and confidence from the fact of going through the motions and sticking up for yourself. In that meeting, I put up some very firm boundaries, and to everyone's credit, from that day forward, they all adhered to them. I got more respect from that day. And it all came from sticking up for myself, quietly, fairly, but most importantly firmly.

Permanent Resident

I needed a change. Sydney life was beginning to drag, and I wanted out of the Sydney office. I'd met a girl who lived in Melbourne and we were getting reasonably serious. Also, the company I worked for had been swallowed up by a huge global conglomerate, and most of the operations were now based in Melbourne. My time limit on most things is around two years; it was now June 2013 and I'd been with the same company since the beginning of 2012. I was getting itchy feet, so I asked for a transfer from Sydney to Melbourne, which was relatively easy to get, and before I knew it, I'd exchanged Sydney Harbour for walks with my girlfriend along the Yarra.

Life was peachy. For about two weeks. And then I received a text message from my girlfriend saying, "Meet me." It was a complete bolt from the blue. I'd only been in Melbourne for two weeks, and I'd been with this girl doing the long-distance thing for about six months. And just like that, she broke up with me. I'd left my social network to come to a new city; I knew very few people. For a little while, I took it a bit rough. But only for a little while. I tend to get it all out, then immediately turn a corner. So, I cried for a day, and then—*bam*—I was done. The switch was flicked. It was time to start another new chapter.

That new chapter started with me applying to get permanent residency in Australia. I had a good friend from China who'd lived in Sydney but recently relocated to Melbourne. She was working for a migration company. She introduced me to her agent who gave me a list of everything I needed to get the permanent residency visa. It became very clear very quickly that it was not going to be an easy process. There was a huge amount of documentation and scrutiny, because in order to get the kind of visa I wanted, I needed my employer to sponsor me. The plus side was, if the company agreed to sponsor me, the process was quite quick. The downside is that you become beholden to that company for an additional two years from when your visa is approved.

Now, having grown up in Nigeria, my mind was always kind of bordering on the edge of certain things; I am always looking for the angle. My wife says to me even now, "You take risks on certain things and yet not on others. But the risks you take are not the usual ones!" Well, I took a risk in the way I got my visa.

Obviously, by now I was an expert in chain of command and introducing ideas in a corporate setting. I was adept at making others feel warm and fuzzy. I'd made sure to do this when I entered the Melbourne office. I come across as a playful person, always giggling and smiling. I often play around like a kid until I need to be something else. I ingratiated myself into the place and got along with everyone.

I went to see HR. I told him I wanted to apply for a PR and I was hoping the company would sponsor me. He was very open to the idea. He sent the request up the line, and everyone was happy to do it. I would cover all the fees, and I just needed them to sign off on certain things. Easy. That was the first part sorted.

Then I had to get all the documentation sorted. Again, I was resourceful. I went back through my employment history, my tennis coaching, my time at the tennis academy in Texas, even things in India and Nigeria. Between my PhD and my current job, I'd completed a certificate in project management. I don't even know why I did it at the time; it was just something I did. But it certainly came in handy for my PR application. The whole thing was above board, but I made sure I tweaked things to skew them towards what I knew the examiners would be looking for.

In the end, I built a library of The History of Kaushik. It was a thing of beauty! I then had HR sign off on a few things, and had my migration agent send through a few things requiring sign offs. I orchestrated the whole thing. The process was seamless. I got my PR in no time. Even the agent said to me, "That's a record!" And she'd been an agent for decades.

Many of my friends had said they weren't even going to try for permanent residency because it was too hard, there was too much involved. But I tried my best to convince them that they could do it. Things had to line up, sure, but all you have to do is persevere and it'll work out. And if it doesn't, it's not meant to be. That said, I don't think perseverance simply springs up in the midst of difficulty. The roots of perseverance must grow in deep in a person. Preparing to persevere is the way we prepare to face the unpredictable.

Meeting Veema

I'd been in Melbourne now for almost six months. After breaking up with my previous girlfriend, I'd been socializing a lot, but there was no-one serious on the horizon. Besides, I was caught up in work and applying for my PR. I had a friend, an Irishman who told me about a dating website. He encouraged me to take a look at it. I thought, "Why not?"

The idea was, you paid for six "kisses", which were basically six messages that you can send to people you fancy. And so I sent the first four out to not much response. But the fifth one, that was the one, because the woman I sent it to is now my wife, Veema. And you know the best thing, she didn't have a photo; all she had was a quote—for the life of me I can't remember what it was—but it piqued my interest. So I sent her a message and we started talking. This went on for about a month or so. Neither of us was in too much of a hurry. After that first month, I had to go to Nigeria for Christmas. When I returned in January, she was off to Mauritius, where she's from. So we were doing a lot of messaging but we still hadn't met in person.

Finally, we met in February in Melbourne Central at, of all places, the Pancake Parlour! We had a wonderful first date. I was open and honest. In true Kaushik style, I rocked up in thongs (something she still tells everyone); and worst of all, they were two sizes too big! I don't know what I was thinking with that move, not putting much emphasis on my appearance. I think I thought, "If she can accept me at my worst, then she might love me at my best."

Something that struck me immediately was that Veema liked to listen. Now, this had traditionally been my domain; I've always been a listener, an observer. I'd never really had or taken many opportunities to talk. But here was this woman who listened, which was very interesting because she was curious and asked questions. That was huge for me.

Amazingly, it didn't twig when she told me that her birthday was 5th August. I just smiled and nodded. But the thing is, that's my mother's birthday too. Talk about warning signs! (I'm joking, I'm joking!) We still laugh about it today. But I didn't realize that first night just how much my life was about to change for the better.

We'd barely been together three months when one morning, we were lying in bed and Veema rolled over to me and said, "Hey, my parents are visiting from Mauritius soon. What do you say your parents come over from India and we'll get engaged?" Which is to say that she proposed to me. That's not really going by the book, but of course, that's just the way I like it.

I looked at the ceiling, I looked at her, looked back at the ceiling. And because of my nature, because I am always very easy-going, I agreed. I didn't really think it through. I didn't overthink it. There was no, "Oh, I haven't spent enough time with this girl. I haven't lived with her. I haven't travelled with her." I didn't think about any of that. And so I just said, "Yep, sounds good."

I called my parents and dropped a bit of a bombshell on them. I could imagine them picking up the phone and there I was on the other end going, "Can you come over? There's this girl and we're getting engaged."

They were taken aback, to say the least. There was a moment of shocked silence, followed by a barrage of rapid-fire questions. Who is this girl? When did this happen? What is her background? Will you buy a house? I had to be straight with them: I didn't know all that much about her. All I did know was that I wanted to marry her. Veema is a Hindu, and my parents insisted on a Hindu engagement. So that is what we had.

A Hindu engagement is not for the fainthearted, with lots of fruits and incense, sandalwood, turmeric. The whole bit. I just Googled temples and found a place in Hoppers Crossing, which I didn't know was a dodgy area. I took one of my best friends to inspect it.

The temple was inside a garage, and the garage was next door to an adult store. Moving from the insalubrious exterior into the garage itself, we were soon surrounded by the many Hindu deities. It was quite the transition, to say the least. I spoke to the priest, who was a bit of a no-nonsense character. I liked that; I like people who are straight with you. He said very plainly: "Give me this many dollars and I'll run the ceremony for you." I said, "Done!"

Of course, I got the third degree when I got home. My mum wanted to know his star sign, his caste, all these technical Hindu questions. I just said to her: "Yes, yes, yes." I was actually just telling her what she wanted to hear, just so we could get on with it. I didn't tell her it was in a garage. And I certainly didn't tell her it was next to an adult store in an unseemly part of town. Veema didn't care either. She said, "As long as you've organized it, I don't really care." She's not religious either.

But her parents were, so we had to tick a few boxes. Also, it turned out that Veema's mum was a Leo as well; that made three of the women in my life, all lions, with birthdays barely days from each other. The three of them are spitting images of each other! I got along with Veema's parents right off. Unfortunately, her dad has passed now. I got to spend some time with them before my parents arrived, which was nice. Veema is the eldest of four daughters, so they've had experience with boyfriends and sons-in-law before. Her dad, before he passed, he would tell her that I was very unique. I took it as a compliment! We got along really well, so I guess it was.

Caption: Veema's mom and dad

But even Veema's mum says that she feels very comfortable with me. Which at first I felt was a bit odd because we didn't say much to each other; her English isn't great, and she spoke mainly French. Still, she was lovely. My parents got along really well with them. They focussed on topics like the wedding date, our star signs, did they align, was the wedding date the right one, all the traditional Hindu stuff.

At last, the day of the engagement party arrived. I invited around 50 friends, most of whom I'd met since coming to Melbourne. Veema invited three friends. It was a great day, despite the dodgy surroundings. I wore traditional Hindu garb, while Veema wore her sari. The priest was there in all his glory. It was actually very beautiful; it was done really well. There was a ring and a necklace, and by the end of it we were engaged. Most importantly, all the parents were happy.

Following the engagement, I wanted to make a nice proposal to Veema; something more formal that the one we'd already had. So I took her to Whitehaven Beach on Hamilton Island. I wanted to put a ring on her finger and make her feel nice from a Western perspective. So, we did that in July.

Veema's birthday is on 5th August. So, we decided 6th August would be the paper wedding in Melbourne. That was a civil service, with no one else in attendance. The parents had all gone home. They'd already set the date for the wedding in October in Mauritius and India. But the paper wedding had to be done first because otherwise Mauritius wouldn't run our wedding in October. A documentation thing. So, we actually had to do like a paper thing in Melbourne.

Itchy Feet

I was now married, and my residency had come through. It all seemed to happen around the same time. A complete change in my life. People dream of staying in developed countries, getting residencies and citizenships. But I couldn't really appreciate it. That's just my nature. When I get something, it's the thrill of trying to get it, the chase, the angles. But then, once I get it, I'm bored and I want to get something else. So, after I got my permanent residency, I was pleased, but I didn't do cartwheels. Some people do cartwheels, but that just isn't me, for better or worse.

But there was a catch. With that residency deal, I had to stay with my company for another two years. My cunning Nigerian brain did not digest that little fact. I just thought to myself, "I've got the PR. Cool. Now I might be a little bit adventurous with the way I'm going to approach life in Australia." Still, I couldn't change companies or jobs because, every time, someone new would have to sponsor me.

At the same time, I felt that I was a free bird in Australia, free to spread my wings and do whatever I like. And then, around August, I realized that all the goals I'd had for myself at the time, the residency, the wedding, it was all done, and now I was bored. I needed some action, another little change somewhere. So I did what I usually do when I feel that way, I decided to write to Australia's leading universities. Just to put the feelers out, see what might come back, what opportunities were out there. I sent up rocket after rocket, just out of curiosity. Who knew where it would lead? I told them who I was and what my experience had been to that point. Nothing came back for a couple of months. But October rolled around and we had the weddings in Mauritius and India. It was also at this time, just prior our wedding travels, that I had to travel to Sri Lanka for work.

Then it was off on the wedding journey. We had a full-blown five-day Hindu ceremony in Mauritius. It was huge. Family and friends flew in from all over the world, including my friends from my PhD years in Sydney. But there was one great sadness for me over that time; my dad was stuck in Nigeria because of the Ebola outbreak. The Mauritius officials were not allowing anyone in from that part of the world. It was terrible, my dad not being able to be there. During the ceremony, seeing him just there on a screen, beaming in via Skype, was too much and I broke down and cried. I wanted him to be there so much. But the silver lining was that I got to see the rest of my family and friends all together to celebrate our wedding. I guess it was a foreshadowing of COVID times, and the difficulties we were all to face in just a few years' time.

It was such a whirlwind. We jetted off to India to do the whole thing again. This time Dad could make it, much to our relief. That was a little more strained because Veema hadn't been to India before, and she didn't like the place. It was too dirty for her, too chaotic. It made her retreat into herself, which strained relations with my family a bit. Anyway, we got through it all and returned home, having had weddings in Melbourne, Mauritius and India.

Once we got home, a few months passed, and then things really started kicking off career-wise. Firstly, I received a random email from the University of Melbourne that said, "Sorry, the email you sent last year slipped through the cracks. Someone's picked it up and they want to speak with you." This was a result of the bunch of emails I'd sent out before we went to Mauritius and India. They wanted to talk to me about a role in the School of Accounting.

Again, I hadn't prepared. I didn't want to prepare. I was happy to wing it. I met with the Dean and a professor. I basically sold them my industry experience. Bear in mind, I'd only had a few years of sustainability-industry experience and limited teaching experience. But I was able to sell it in a positive way. I didn't realize what I was doing, but I just kept going.

At last, one of them said, "Okay. Here's what we're offering you. We're going to give you a course called Sustainability Accounting. You will teach in semester two. And you're going to coordinate the course as well as set the exam. Are you up for the challenge?"

Again, in the same way as when Veema proposed to me, me being me, I just shrugged and said, "Yep, all good. Piece of cake. Done."

I took the job. I'd never marked a paper before. I'd never coordinated a course before. I didn't realize how intense it was going to be.

It was around this time that we went on a trip to Kangaroo Island in South Australia. I remember, we were on a ferry and I just had that feeling of existential boredom again. I needed to change things up. So, right there on the water I downloaded the Seek app. Normally, when looking to see what's out there, I type in "sustainability." But this time, I decided to type "corporate citizenship."

My mind went back to my PhD, when I was visiting many companies and had great relationships with them. At the time, the wife of the guy I was doing research assistant work for held a Corporate Citizenship Director role at a global consulting firm. I'd built a good relationship with her husband via my PhD. I knew by now that sustainability had many different iterations. You can call it sustainability, corporate social responsibility, corporate citizenship, so many things.

So, I typed in "corporate citizenship" and a job came up, Corporate Citizenship Manager at this particular firm. And I thought, "Oh, I know someone there. In fact, I know the husband of the lady recruiting for that role, probably." Right there on that ferry, I sent off a text message to the guy I was doing RA work for saying, "I've seen this role. Can you let me know what you think?" He replied in two minutes and he said, "I've just spoken to my wife. She wants you to call her on Monday."

Monday morning rolled around, we were back in Melbourne. I made the call and she said, "Kaushik, you called at the right time because we are about to close the applications. We've got one person in mind, but why don't you throw your hat in the ring?" And so I did it. I applied. She spoke to HR and basically fast-tracked my application, got me to an interview.

Now, my then employer and this new place were competitors. There was a non-compete clause in my contract, which would preclude me from taking up a position with the competition. As fortune would have it, though, the new gig was not client-facing; it was internal. I was to build the climate change sustainability strategy for the company, not for our clients. Which meant I wasn't going to be in direct competition with my current employer. The role was perfect; it ticked every box. And so, I got offered the job. The pay was eye-opening, for me at least. It was the first time I'd entered into a six-figure salary. It was nearly double what I was making currently. I think of it as a great leap forward.

My superiors tried to make me feel bad for leaving, but I just had to get out of there. I have no regrets. I signed in early June of that year, while also signing with a Melbourne university to teach part-time in late May. I called my new employer and said, "I need to teach part-time one night a week. Are you cool with that?" And they had to check with the audit partner from a risk point of view, because the university was a client of theirs. But everything came back fine and I was good to go. Which means I'd gone from one job which I was somewhat bored with, to going to Sri Lanka, to realizing I love travelling, to finding a job in another massive firm, which was all on my merit, not through an acquisition, while also landing a massive academic brand. It was a wonderful, fulfilling time.

Corporate Citizen

Once again, although I'd landed the new role, I didn't have experience in the area they'd hired me for. I knew sustainability, of course, but I'd more or less always been client-facing. They wanted me to build an internal strategy for the company. That involved stakeholder engagement, influencing, lobbying, navigating through office politics, playing a significant political game with leadership, basically sifting through the entire company. Once again it was time to wing it!

I was pleased to get the gig, because this new company was a great brand, but also I'd landed the job through my own efforts, my wits, contacts and experience. That meant a lot to me. I'm better at being in-house, dealing with internal politics. My role was to build a strategy for them around climate change. They were doing a lot of work in that space with clients. Globally, they were doing a lot of work on their own footprint, but in Australia there wasn't much focus there. I joined them as Manager of Corporate Citizenship, which was a broad title, as opposed to manager of climate change or sustainability manager. Corporate citizenship has more of a social touch to it.

During my almost three years there, we launched our first ever climate change strategy, which included a whole range of targets. We won a whole bunch of awards in that sustainability space. We actually won the first ever sustainability award for the company. We were featured as case studies in many publications for our work in that environment, climate change space, but I guess my key learning at that time was in engaging with the key stakeholders within the company, who were spread between Melbourne and Sydney. I had to figure out for myself, how I would get in front of these key people. How do I form bonds? How do I get these conversations going? How do I build those relationships?

I still remember a senior C-suite executive at the time. His attitude was, "I'm not all that interested in sustainability, but if it can save me money, then great." I wanted him to be the sponsor of this strategy, because then you've got someone controlling the dollars, controlling the operations. So when I heard his tone of voice, and realized I'd have a bit of a task getting him on-board, it was a bit deflating.

I was bringing in something new. But at first the business was scared about its sudden appearance, and mine along with it. I realized pretty quickly I wasn't going to have the immediate support I'd assumed I'd have.

I made it my first job to become very good friends with all the personal assistants, because it was all about forming a partnership. There were around 400 partners across the country, and they each had a personal assistant. Also, the directors had PAs. They were the ones who'd get me meetings with senior people. Befriending those PAs was key to getting a foot in the door.

I had to be careful. As I'd learned before, sometimes my bosses didn't like me directly contacting their bosses. My current boss, who was then a partner, at first seemed a little sensitive around this, but she also understood where I was going with this. At least someone did! I didn't really have a plan. I was, as always, winging it.

But I did author the strategy, which soon enough became my baby. It was the company's first ever climate change strategy (did I already mention this?). I am proud of that, especially given the static I received early on. I'm proud of the ways I managed to reduce that static, and how I worked through it. Climate change became my area. Anytime someone thought about the environment or climate change, or wanted to roll out an initiative, they would come to me. That was so nice. I'd found a place there, my place.

Finding the Sweet Spot

I soon started teaching at university. I remember going into my first class, I was not nervous at all. My wife was probably more nervous than I was. It was a massive auditorium. Students were filing in, and I just stood there. I had my slides ready to go. It was my very first time standing in front of a class as a lecturer. I looked around the room. Okay, so maybe I was nervous for 10 seconds. But in those 10 seconds I was just observing, I understood the lay of the land and I saw more nervousness from the students than me.

My first priority was to ask students what this word "sustainability" meant to them. Then I asked how many were here because they had to be, because it was a mandatory class. These questions just popped in my head. I didn't script it. I didn't plan or rehearse. 99% of the cohort raised their hands and said they had to be there because it was a requirement for their degree. (It is worth noting I asked the same question at the end of the semester and 99% wished they had raised their hand because they wanted to be there!)

That first semester, I had a lot of fun. My rating was good, something like 4.9 out of five from student feedback. It was, apparently, a record. The main gist was that I was very likeable. I think, really, it was because I enjoyed teaching so much. I was able to connect with the students. Being grounded in practical experience, I brought a lot of industry knowledge into my lectures. The students seemed to appreciate that. It wasn't just dry theory. This harked back to my tennis coaching days, everything I'd been through in terms of both being coached and being a coach. I knew it from both sides. Which meant I knew how to get ideas across, what the roadblocks would be, and the best methods for helping students to absorb the information.

I remember one student from that class, a Chinese girl who always sat at the front. When we first went around the class doing introductions, she said she was an accountant in Beijing who'd come to do her Master's.

Six months after our class finished, she wrote to me telling me that because of my class, she'd changed careers and gone to work in climate change and sustainability in Beijing. That was lovely to hear, and very satisfying to the teacher in me.

I taught at that university for three years. Fortunately, I've always been good at time management. People always wonder how I fit so many things into my life. I clock in and out at a certain time every day, because I always have more than one thing to attend to. There's always an eye on something else. If I've had time away from my wife for teaching, I'll always find a way to make it up to her. Fairness and balance are integral to the way I operate. Also, I had to ensure the teaching didn't take time away from my day job.

I always found a way to make time for Veema. It was a conscious effort on my part to ensure that she was more important to me than work. So I had to find that balance. And I loved teaching. That's probably what made it a little bit easier to do that one night of teaching each week. I would look forward to it. It was a good balance between the corporate and the academic work, because when I teach, it's like I'm getting therapy from my students. It cuts both ways.

Sometimes in class I'd go off on a rant about my day-to-day at work; I'd tell them about some sort of challenge or crisis we had and how we solved it. Then I'd ask them what they thought about it. Their responses were always so much different to the ones I got at the corporate level. Often, I'd go back to corporate and take these young, sometimes naïve insights, which were actually quite amazing. They proved to be quite useful!

I'd found my sweet spot. It was 9-5 corporate, 6-9 teaching. If I could teach once a week, I would have attained self-actualization.

The balance was just right. If I was a bit unsure what was I trying to achieve with my climate change strategy, or if I was finding things difficult there, I'd walk into that classroom and feel a layer of confidence like a shield around me. And that's the thing, all these experiences like joining a fraternity in the US, playing college tennis, coaching tennis—it all gave me a confidence that I never knew I had in me. I wasn't brought up to feel confident because my performance and person was always scrutinized. It was rarely positive, it was always, "You can do more, you can do this, you can do that!"

But my students looked up to me. They saw what I was doing, both at the university and in the corporate world, and saw a model for their own career paths. Also, Veema would say to me, "My whole family looks up to you. You're very unique. Your background, like being able to do a PhD, being a professional tennis player, working in sustainability, it's such a huge achievement!" She said her family in Mauritius looked up to me, and they wanted to know more about me because I'd only been there once. This kind of thing made me feel that it's all worthwhile. It also made me feel confident in myself. After all the things I'd been through in my younger years, confidence wasn't something that came naturally, so to have anything that added to my confidence was a godsend. And confidence is cumulative; when you have a bit of belief in yourself, you'll try new things, and when you see that it's okay to try new things, you'll try even more, and when those things work out, or you at least learn something from your efforts, your knowledge base and confidence will grow and grow. The trouble is, a lot of us get stuck in our routine or patterned way of doing things; sometimes we acquire the know-how for a certain job, task or skill, but lack the "do-how" to actually put these things into action. But just like know-how, you can also acquire do-how!

Lesson 14: A Do-How Deficit

Know-how is a common commodity. Most people know how to do their jobs, and if they lack specific skills, they acquire them through research, classes, reading, training seminars or advice from others. Knowing how is not the tough part. Problems arise when people discover that they can't translate their know-how into the do-how they need to accomplish their plans and achieve their goals.

Before you can begin to translate know-how into do-how, you must clearly identify your goals. When firm objectives are in place, people or companies can plan orderly steps for productive, results-oriented action. Failure to set new goals often stems from ingrained "habits, culture and choices." People operate according to habitual thought patterns that, while largely opaque to the thinker, prove inordinately powerful and resistant to change. Often, real change cannot take place until people find a way to recognize and put aside or transcend their customary ways of thinking. When it comes to organizations, their familiar ways of transacting business and the routine thinking that underlies it, are often very resistant to change. The transition from know-how to do-how is never easy, but it is learnable.

The "Do-How Map"

The "Do-How Map" can help you make behavioural breakthroughs by discovering and avoiding the limiting hidden rules that hamper your thoughts and actions. The breakthrough cycle activates when an "idea leads to practice leads to insight leads to a breakthrough."

The map has four steps:

1. *Recognize Your Do-How Moments*

   Do-how moments can cause notable anxiety because they occur outside your comfort zone. You may experience fear, anger, frustration, sadness or any other negative emotion. Recognize these feelings as helpful signposts that you are at a crossroads: a do-how moment. This is the time to block the hidden rules that normally manipulate your thinking. Take the time to reflect: stop, look and choose the best response. Don't simply act. Think first, so you can step courageously out of your comfort zone and select a new path.

2. *Spell out the Breakthrough You Want*

Be precise and ambitious when you plan your desired outcome. Specify the way you want to respond to the reality you now confront, including how you will think and behave. Use the "Four P's": "picture" the desired breakthrough and describe it in totally "positive" language; be "precise" about the way your desired breakthrough looks, sounds and feels. Ask yourself, if everything is "possible," what is the one thing you want to make totally attainable?

3. *Uncover Your Hidden Rules*

Try to get in touch with your embedded assumptions, even though it isn't easy, and examine how they affect your thinking. Your hidden rules are stories you tell yourself, for example, "People don't like me" and "Things always go wrong." Don't automatically accept that the narratives of your hidden rules are true. They are mental shortcuts, nothing more. To find your hidden rules, consider what you avoid, what makes you uncomfortable and in which areas you are strong. Be willing to feel a little unnerved in order to identify your hidden rules.

4. *Take Responsibility for Your Choices*

You aren't a victim; you are in charge of your life, your choices, your behaviour and your actions. Don't blame others—or circumstances—for your choices. The next time you confront a problem, solve it yourself. Ask yourself, "How do I want things to be?" and then decide, "What can I do now to take responsibility for getting the results I want?" Everybody knows that change is difficult, but it doesn't have to be complicated.

Switching on Efficiency

Sometimes, I would still receive pushback from my bosses. I wasn't getting validation from them. The way I countered this was not to go over their heads, but to look outside the company for validation. If we could be recognized in the community for doing great work, if I could show our efforts to the world and have the world take notice, then my bosses would start to see the value in what I was doing.

And that's what I did. I looked into what the firm was doing around the world, and started building a foundation to capture all the great work that had already been done and adding reports stating work that needed still to be done. I had a buddy who looked after a program that helped buildings be more energy efficient. They were an emerging initiative and were offering an award to companies that were doing amazing work in this space. It seemed perfect for us. So I sent in an application for a national sustainability award.

This award was trying to build its profile as well at the time. What better way to build a profile than giving an award to a huge player like the company I worked for? We had to be worthy winners, of course. But, to be honest, I put together a strong application because of the great work that we had already done. The recycling rates, the energy efficiency we achieved, the cost reductions, paper reductions. We had saved something like five Eiffel Towers worth of paper! I packaged it all up and sent it off. And, would you believe it, we won! This put me in touch with Lord Mayors in both Sydney and Melbourne; it expanded my network and further ingratiated the business into the sustainability space.

To be clear, though, I wasn't doing a lot of the logistical legwork with regards to sustainability initiatives. I was packaging it up. It was about working smart. I wasn't putting a solar panel on the roof. I wasn't implementing all these technologies, many of which were coming from our clients. We would be in a building that's run by companies that have big sustainability credentials. Because of them, we would have to recycle, we would have six different bins; because of them, not because of us, we'd have solar panels on the roof. And so I piggybacked off their work. It was all above board, but I saw an opportunity to capitalize on work that was already being done. And, at long last, my C-suite executive came to me and said, "Oh, we won an award did we?" I said, "Yep!" And he said, "This is going to the board!"

Following which, the internal resistance started to drop off. My job became a lot easier because of that external validation. My boss's boss loved it. She just loved that we won that award. So it was a win-win; we were being validated externally, and I was being validated internally.

I also started talking at conferences around this time. I hadn't done any public speaking engagements until now. There was a social enterprise that dealt with food waste. They worked with restaurants, and they collected any leftovers for companies whose workers were hungry. Busy workers could find a meal, pay a discounted price, go pick it up. They were in their pilot phase at the time. They asked me if they could partner with us. I jumped on it. Now it's a massive success. At the time they asked me to speak at the Melbourne Food and Wine Festival. I jumped on that too. I have a mind to jump on every opportunity that presents itself. At the Festival, it was a strong panel made up of a MasterChef, a senior political party leader, a guy from a radio show and a lady who was on the next Mars mission. I was going along to talk about food waste. It was a runaway success. And so, from then on, I looked out for similar opportunities. I spoke at waste conferences and energy conferences and sustainability conferences, all in an effort to make me more effective within the company, to give me more clout, if you like. An added bonus was that I was developing my own personal brand. I didn't intend this, it wasn't so calculated as all that, but I was making a name for myself, so I kept speaking. I'd have audiences of 10, I'd have audiences of 100. Sometimes I'd have audiences of 500 at conferences in the Melbourne Convention Centre and the Sydney Convention Centre.

Caption: my first business conference presentation in Sydney, Australia

Caption: recent conference presentation with one of my largest audiences

Lesson 15: On Seizing Opportunities

Opportunities Come and Go

When an opportunity presents itself, knowing that it may not come back helps you stay vigilant and aware. You need to continually be on the lookout for great opportunities that you want to take advantage of.

You Will Look Back and Appreciate Them

Think back on those times when you went out of your comfort zone and pursued an opportunity. I am so proud of the opportunities I have seized on my journey. Especially the ones that I had to find for myself.

You Are Stretching Yourself and Growing

Part of having a growth mindset is to believe that learning is crucial. Those times when you don't feel 100% confident that you can do something, but you still go out and seize the opportunity, are very rewarding.

Learn to Identify Excellent Opportunities for Yourself

When you get into the habit of pursuing the opportunities you want, you develop an eye for them. You spend a lot of time thinking about what you want and how you can get what you want.

You Are Setting a Good Example

Every day, I remind myself that my actions are bigger than me and serve as my legacy. There are many lessons that I would like to pass to the next generation, and this is one of them. Don't wait for things to happen to you; pursue what you want. Unless you map out a detailed picture of what you want and combine that with action, you'll veer off-path and bypass great opportunities.

So, here's what you need to do:

Step 1: Think About an Area of Your Life You'd Like to Change for the Better

Imagine what it would feel and look like if you were able to change this area of your life. Think about the best possible outcome/scenario that could occur if everything were to go exactly the way you want it to go (it never goes perfectly, but don't worry about that right now).

Step 2: Take this Vision and Write it Down as a Goal

Be as detailed and specific as possible.

Step 3: Break that Goal Down into Several Small Steps

If you're not sure what steps you need to take to achieve your goal, then your first step is to start reading, researching, and gathering knowledge about what you need to do. You might need to talk to someone who's already done what you want to do or find an inspiring podcast that can help fast-track your way to success.

The main idea is this: you need to decide on some sort of action you can right now to make progress on your goal.

Some examples: Want to start a business? Start researching how to get a business license. Want a new car? Go to the car dealership and test drive that car you want. Do something, anything, to get the ball rolling.

Step 4: Remain Consistent and Keep Taking Action

Once you've taken one small step towards your goal, you'll need to set up another one. And another one. And another one. Along the way, you'll notice different ideas and opportunities that you can leverage towards achieving your goal.

Outside My Comfort Zone

My public speaking was ramping up. I was winning awards and starting up some solid sustainable initiatives. I got in touch with the people at a global not-for-profit organization. I'd noticed that our catering team used a lot of their fair trade products. So I contacted them after noticing that they certified various companies who used their products. It would be great branding. I asked if we were in the running for certification. He looked at how much we spent on their products every year. Lo and behold, we became certified as one of the top fair trade companies! It also led to the people from that company asking me to join their board, which I gleefully accepted. I was newly married, working in corporate sustainability, engaging as a public speaker, teaching at university, I'd also been asked to guest lecture and mentor at another university, and was now on the board at a global not-for-profit organization. But, naturally, in true Kaushik style, things were about to change. I was young and hungry, and to be honest, I was taking on a lot and often caught myself wanting to do too much and expecting results too quickly. After a long time in the corporate world, I can tell you that there is much to be said for taking things at a measured speed and learning to pace yourself.

Caption: Delivering a masterclass for Rotary Club

Lesson 16: On the Importance of Pacing Yourself

Often when we're young, just beginning our adult journey, we feel as though we have to do everything at once. We need to decide everything, plan out our lives, experience everything, get to the top, find true love, figure out our life's purpose, and do it all at the same time.

Slow down. Don't rush into things. Let your life unfold. Wait a bit to see where it takes you, and take time to weigh your options. Enjoy every bite of food, take time to look around you, let the other person finish their side of the conversation. Allow yourself time to think, to mull a bit. Taking action is critical. Working towards your goals and making plans for the future is commendable and often very useful. But rushing full-speed ahead towards anything is a one-way ticket to burnout and a good way to miss your life as it passes you by.

Caption: Golden Bridge in Vietnam

Walking Away

In any job, there will come a time, a moment, when you know it's time to move on. For me, this usually happens within a couple of years, sometimes less. Even with my first job in Corporate Sustainability, after the first week I had an eye out for other positions. I didn't want to leave, necessarily, but I'm always curious to know what's out there. Sometimes I take that curiosity even further. Within a week of starting in CS I took a meeting with some people at one of Australia's largest food companies, based in Sydney. And not long after that, I threw my hat into the ring when a position opened up within the Auckland Council in New Zealand. I actually landed that job, they offered it to me, but ultimately I declined it. It wasn't a step forward; it was more a step sideways to a similar role in a different location. If you're going to make a change, make it work for you.

As you might have gathered, I don't have a five-year or a 10-year career plan; I'm actually not that ambitious or career-driven. Instead, I like to have challenges along the way. Can I actually get that job and go through the process? Because I love doing interviews, I did a few within a short period of joining the CS world. Not because I wanted the job but because I got a rush from it!

At one point an AFL club came knocking. They wanted to talk to me about an opening as General Manager for Community Engagement. The CEO wanted to have a chat with me. I thought, "Why not?"

So I went in all suited up, did the interview. I made it through to the final round, for which I was interviewed by three executives at the club. But ultimately I lost out to someone more experienced in the space. I was glad for that, to be honest. I was lucky not to go down that road.

But, once I get the feeling that a job has run its course for me, that feeling is parked away somewhere. The longest I've stayed at any single company is three years. If it isn't right, I'm happy to walk away after a week, to a better opportunity. Soon enough that feeling lodged inside me in my role. I didn't like knowing that I was going to be stuck at a particular salary band for the foreseeable future, going to be stuck in this position, because no one's going to leave above me. There were only two people above me and they weren't going anywhere. They'd both been with the company for about 20 years each. My boss basically summed it up by saying, "You've put us on the map for climate change and environment." That was my dot on the page. That was the tiny bit of the company that I could impact on. Which meant, there wasn't all that much else for me to do.

Towards the end of 2017, I was a bit over two years into the role. By now I was bored. One day, I went on Jobs and I saw an advert for a Sustainability Analyst with one of Australia's largest aged care companies. I'd never heard of them before, and I never wanted to be an analyst, that was too junior, and yet I applied for it.

Within an hour I got a call from their HR person, who said, "Hey Kaushik, I'm just checking in to see if you know what you applied for? I don't know why you've applied for it, because I've just seen your resumé." I knew I was overqualified, but as usual I was putting the feelers out there. As we were talking—I hadn't planned this at all—I shifted gears; I told her that I knew what the advertised role was, but I had another idea. I pitched her a different role, one I knew well, and one that would serve their company well. I created this opportunity out of thin air. I hadn't even researched the company. Nevertheless, we clicked and she went away saying she would have an internal discussion about my proposal.

A week later she came back to me with an invitation to come into the office for an interview. I didn't know what I wanted out of it; I just went for the interview. We all sat down and they asked me about the ideas I had for their company. Once again, I winged it. I said, "Oh, without being like Martin Luther King, I have a vision."

Now, I didn't know aged care had yet to move into sustainability. I was going to be their first ever dedicated sustainability professional. I didn't know any of that at the time. I didn't know what the salary expectation was. I described the role I'd have within their firm, and what the benefits of that would be. Then they asked me, "Okay, and what do you expect as a salary?" What I said was significantly more than what I was expecting! It was a way of making it worth my while. They baulked a little at that, but didn't refuse it outright. It was the beginning of a negotiation, and I was eager to see where it went.

I didn't hear from them for a month. Then they wanted another meeting, this time with the General Manager who was coming down from Queensland. I met with him, and we gelled pretty well straight away. I re-pitched the position to him. And the salary.

All he said was, "Do you know why this role was created?" I said, "Why?" He said, "The CEO's son has been pestering him to do something about sustainability. He's been doing it for two years and so we created this role." I said, "Did you cut and paste it from somewhere?" He said, "Yeah." I said, "Okay, so you've got everything you need from me?" He said, "Yeah."

Then I said, "When will you let me know, because I'm about to go on a six-week holiday to India, Mauritius, Egypt and Jordan, and the last thing I want is to miss something when I'm overseas." He said, "Oh, you'll be notified in two weeks."

Now, at the same time I was also chasing something in Amsterdam. I'd had a chat with the head of global sustainability at the company I was currently working for. By the time I met with the aged care company representatives in Melbourne, I'd had two telephone meetings with the Amsterdam people. After the second one, they decided I wasn't right for the role, but they did tell me that there was something else coming up they thought I'd be perfect for.

The day I told the aged care company that I was off for a six-week holiday, I got a call from Amsterdam saying, "There's a role for you in Amsterdam. I've already interviewed you so I know what you can do. Just give me a couple of weeks to come back to you."

There was no avoiding it, I'd have to wait for both, and it was likely I'd be notified about both while I was away.

We went to India first, spending two weeks with my parents. That was a beautiful time. I think that was Veema's last time visiting India actually. Then we went to Egypt and Jordan. I hadn't heard anything for either of my prospective employers.

We were in Mauritius when the call came through from Amsterdam. They were offering me a job, but it was all a bit vague. They wanted me to return to Melbourne first, then they'd sort out the internal stuff, how to organize my transfer from Australia to Holland. It didn't fill me with hope, although I was leaning that way over the aged care place. I wanted more global exposure, a chance in another country for a while.

The very next morning I received an email from the aged care company with an informal contract and it said, "You've got the gig. Permanent full-time. Give us a buzz if you have any questions."

Veema came in, I showed her the email and she was shocked. Then my mother-in-law came in and we showed it to her. She was so shocked she had to sit down. For us, the offer was incredible; it was an incredible amount of money, we hadn't seen such sums of money before. Not that it was completely about the money. But it was impressive.

Still, I didn't leap on it. I wanted to pause. I told my wife, let's pause, finish our holiday. Let's think about it when we get back to Australia.

We finished our time in Mauritius by flying on a helicopter and visiting an underwater waterfall. We also went on safari and played with some cheetahs and lions. It was all very memorable.

We came back to Australia and I still hadn't signed anything. I was thinking it all over. In the meantime, my junior had left. On the surface, this was fine. Those sorts of things happened. After all, I was in the throes of leaving too. But on the back of her resignation, they had asked me to fly up to Sydney. I got on a flight, went to Sydney, didn't realize what I was going into. I walked into the office, my boss pulled me into a meeting room and said, "Don't take this as bad feedback. And please don't leave us. What I'm about to tell you, please don't take it in a bad way." That caught me on the back foot right off.

Then they got to the problem: "We received some feedback from this person about your management skills." Basically, they were blaming me for my junior's resignation. They were a bit harsh to me in that meeting. They didn't even seem to want to hear my side of things.

While it was all going on, all I could think of was, "I can't wait for this to be over, because I've got something to share with you." They kept going on about what they had to say, while I was becoming more and more indignant.

After this meeting was over, I went to Star City Casino to have lunch. I called the aged care company and signed the contract.

I didn't tell my employer right away. I came back to Melbourne that night, I told Veema the good news. She was over the moon.

The next day, I called my boss in Sydney. She said, "Don't tell me you're leaving." I said, "I am indeed leaving. I'm leaving for a job that's giving me a significant pay rise. I'm going into another job with a much larger remit."

It's important to note I wasn't burning a bridge. We are still friends. We meet for dinner often. The way that I laid it out to her was, "I need to progress. It's very unfortunate the way that it was delivered, but there are no hard feelings regarding the feedback, but I am going somewhere that I think is a better fit for me at this stage."

After that I called my contact in Amsterdam and told them I'd accepted another offer. That was a very memorable shift for me, from a career perspective. From there I entered my next stint in aged care.

Learning to Take Feedback and Criticism

The feedback I received in that final meeting was tough to take. They were levelling accusations at me, while I felt they hadn't really understood the full story. Even more frustrating, I wasn't asked to provide my side of the argument; they just went into delivery mode. For a long time, I have struggled with criticism. Of course, you're going to get feedback wherever you go, especially at work. But for me, particularly because of the abuse I'd suffered in school, I'd become very sensitive to it. It's certainly something I've had to work on.

Having a contract in hand with the aged care company no doubt softened the blow. Had I not had that, I don't know how I would have taken it. But I remained silent, and resolved to simply take the criticism and look forwards to better days.

These days, I always ask for feedback, especially from my juniors. When I get feedback, I always listen. I never take it as an accusation, but I always apply the fairness principle.

If the feedback you've been given is well thought out and fair, then you must cope with it, listen to what's being said and try to absorb as much as you can; because we're all human, we can all improve in one way or another. But in this instance, I felt hard done by. I think it could have been handled a lot better. Especially from my boss, with whom I was good friends. To hear criticism put so bluntly, hurt. Sometimes I felt that I was at the global consulting firm just out of loyalty to my ultimate boss, not to the brand, because she had been lovely to me. That's the thing my wife doesn't get about me, sometimes I'm so loyal to people who are not only the best, but because they'd done some little, sweet deed or something for me; it means a lot.

My boss was good to me. She took part in my PhD; she gave me some very helpful insights. And her husband had given me a job, so all that mattered to me. We shared a connection, but to be hauled over the coals like that was too much. I made my decision and didn't look back.

Switching Industries

And so, I took up my new position at an aged care company as their National Sustainability Manager. It was something of a shock to begin with, from being used to the flashy buildings in the CBD, I walked into this little office in Melbourne. It was clear I was going to have to adjust my expectations.

But some things remained the same. During my first week on the job we were all attending a charity lunch. I was standing in the queue for sandwiches behind a man who would have been in his late-60s or early 70s. I recognised him as the CEO, though I was yet to meet him. I introduced myself, saying, "Hi, I'm Kaushik, I'm the new sustainability guy." Bear in mind, it was his son that pushed for my role within the company.

This guy barely batted an eyelid. He said, "Oh, nobody told me you'd been hired." I asked him if I could get half an hour of his time for a chat. He was a bit rough around the edges. He agreed, but put me off for about two weeks. When eventually we did sit down, I put forward my ideas in broad terms (I didn't know what I was doing), and he basically said, "Kaushik, this is my company, so if you come in here with any of your 'save the planet' palaver, before you know it you and this programme will cease to exist, before it even started." At least I knew what I was up against!

This was an ASX100 company at the time, so they were a reasonably big company. But it was run as a family business.

In my field of work, it is important to take a measured approach. If you're too passionate, if you go in all guns blazing and flags flying, you've lost half the battle, because your passion will overpower pragmatism. You won't change the world. You have to focus on that tiny dot in the centre of the page. You also have to be aware that being mindful of sustainability just isn't for everyone; people have different priorities. It pays to put yourself in other people's shoes.

In my response that day, I was careful to show him that I understood where he was coming from. Then I outlined the kinds of things I'd done before, and the positive effects those things had had on the companies I'd worked for. I also made it clear that of all the work I've done, none of it has been achieved by stepping on anyone's toes. If I could set him at ease and make him feel in control of the situation, it would make my life a hell of a lot easier. At the end of the meeting, I said, "I promise you that I'll repay you my salary 10 times over in the first two years." Bold, but it raised his eyebrows.

I was there for just over two years (more or less my limit). In those two years, I spent the first three months travelling around Australia, to 50 of their 67 sites. I conducted lots of workshops in an effort to understand what their sites wanted, what their clinical facility managers, staff, etc., wanted from sustainability.

Meanwhile, I was developing a sustainability strategy that looked into solar energy and the installation of LED lights across the board. I was good with financials, and ultimately I had one of the largest budgets in the company.

In my first year alone, we installed some 25,000 LED bulbs and over three gigawatts of solar across the country.

At first, my boss challenged me. "You know the CEO will never sign off on your strategy, never. Because your strategy is game-changing for aged care. He wouldn't do anything like that. He's a safe bet kind of guy." My boss bet me; he said, "I'll buy you a beer if you can get it done before this date."

There was another big issue at that juncture. My employment coincided with the Royal Commission into Aged Care. People were nervous, and there was the whiff of change—and not just small change—in the air. It made my job more difficult, because people were reluctant to make any changes before they had to.

In any case, what we didn't know was that the CEO was about to resign. But two months before he did, I got him to sign off on the strategy (my boss graciously took me out for a beer). That was a huge win; along the way I'd been implementing projects, handling loads of internal problems, lots of lobbying, and (as always) maintaining an excellent relationship with my boss's PA.

By travelling to our sites, meeting the people on the ground, I had built a lot of trust with the staff all around the country. I always took the approach that I was not there to change the world. I was not there to plant some trees. I was also not just there to save them money. It was a balanced approach, which everyone from the ground up understood. Also when you're likeable and relatable, it makes life a little bit easier.

One of my prouder moments was just before our CEO resigned, when he pulled me to the side and said, "You know, I've never fully understood what you do here, or why you came into the business, but now you've piqued my interest and got me thinking. You have achieved what you wanted to achieve in one and a half years, so kudos to you."

Then (surprise, surprise), he gave me a hug! I was dumbfounded. This, from the man who was feared across the business. Nobody expected that from him, and certainly not me. This CEO was very old-school, old fashioned values, and a bit of a man's man. And now here he was hugging the guy from sustainability! That was really nice. That was a year and a half, but I also sensed that it was the changing of the guard. Change was afoot, and I was wondering what that spelled for me.

As with my former job, I was eager to put us up for as many awards as we could win. And we did win some. We quickly became the leader in the field in terms of sustainability. If you talked about sustainability in aged care, you had to talk about us. We were in all the media, so I was doing a lot of the comms, we'd chat to all the journalists. As always, I was very proactive, and I was lucky, because they basically made me the spokesperson for the company on sustainability. That gave me a lot of exposure; I received invitations to do public talks. I'd made that role for myself; that was my brand. Initially, they wanted someone to come in, crunch some numbers and plug in some light bulbs. But what ended up happening is they got a guy who became the face of sustainability for the company, embedded it across the business, across supply chain, across HR, across marketing and comms, across the facilities.

Even now, I still get photos sent to me from the lifestyle team about all the stuff they're doing around sustainability at a site level. I love that. It's satisfying to remember that, unlike at other places I've worked, there was no team; it was just me and my boss. We just winged it.

Politics? No Thanks.

I'd met a senior political leader on a panel about food put together by a global not-for-profit organization. On a whim, I emailed him to learn about his policies on sustainability. He was very open to talking about it and invited me into his office for a chat. Afterwards, he invited me to a private dinner to meet the party's "inner sanctum". What I didn't realize at the time was that I was being groomed to run for councillor or some similar position within the party. Before the dinner, they sent two councillors to our home for a meeting with Veema and I. But by the end of the dinner, while sitting next to some people from Canberra, I was quickly turned off by what I was seeing.

It wasn't my game. It all seemed a bit wishy-washy. This politician who'd invited me came by and said, "Hey, Kaushik, did you get everything you needed?" I said, "Yeah, thank you very much." He left and then I left and that was it. That was my first and last venture into politics. I wanted to see if it had anything to offer me, and if I had anything to offer it. While I might have been good at politics in the workplace, I wasn't interested in throwing my hat into that arena, not by a long shot.

Pro Bono

It's crucial to be curious. Who knows where your curiosity might take you. Just like with dipping my toe into politics, I often enjoy feeling out situations or unknown experiences. Sometimes (as with politics) it goes nowhere; sometimes it's surprising where it goes. But always, I learn something.

To this end, I have often given talks and public speeches on a pro bono basis. Some people ask why I would do it and not get paid. It's true, often there's a bit of work that needs to go into these talks. But, if it's the right fit for me, I don't necessarily think that being paid is the highest priority. Sometimes it's just good to do these things and trust that, if you're looking for a payoff, it will come to fruition sometime down the road.

For example, I did a talk at a university conference and there was a lady in the audience from yet another Melbourne university. She said, "Hey Kaushik, I love what you did." She then explained that she ran an accelerator program at her university. She explained that they brought a bunch of start-ups together, gave them some money, and taught them various subjects to see if they could successfully launch their businesses. She wanted me to talk about sustainability in start-ups, as a guest lecturer.

I did it for free. Then, six months later, she asked if I could do another. I said, "Yeah, okay." After this she explained that they were interested in my becoming a mentor to some of these start-ups. Now I said I'd do it, but I'd need to be paid. After the work I'd done already, they knew who I was and why I was of value to them. We'd also established a good rapport. So it wasn't unreasonable that I would now be engaged on a more professional basis. She said to me, "Name your price!"

My role was to sit with the students over two four-hour sessions and help them solve a problem. Perhaps it was their value proposition, or their financial or marketing plan, or they wanted to prepare for an upcoming pitch, or it might have been something to do with sustainability.

In fact, the course wasn't really sustainability focussed, and so again, I'd never done this before, I had never built a business or anything like that, so it's something else that I winged. I think I ended up mentoring about 30 start-ups over two and a half years.

Part Five

Covid and Beyond

Redundancy: How to Bounce Back

I kept up with my public speaking. I'd engage on all sorts of topics: sustainability, my personal story, bullying, tennis, travel, a lot about jobs and careers, the life/work balance. My inclination to wing it, and the variety of experiences and pursuits this resulted in, meant that I had a deep reserve of material on which to draw for a host of speaking gigs. I had done a lot in a relatively short time, and I found that people wanted to hear about it. My confidence grew with each appearance. And with my teaching and mentoring at university level, I was becoming quite used to being out in front of people. This really nourished the extrovert side of me.

Meanwhile, I was relishing my work at the aged care company. It was my show—at least my side of it was—and I had almost complete autonomy. I got to create my own little baby, as opposed to being managed closely. Before, I was really the only sustainability guy, whereas now I was in a team. Here it was just me, the whole business was being guided by me. Everyone would come to me for various investor-related issues, ASX issues, aged care, all sorts of things. It was satisfying being respected for my background and education. I hadn't really experienced that before.

I kept travelling all over the countryside, visiting various sites. As I've said, I'd saved my employer a few million dollars in the first couple of years from the projects that I implemented, which was indeed ten times my salary. We'd won many sustainability awards, which meant that we were the *it* company for healthcare and sustainability. I was getting invited to speak at all sorts of conferences and forums.

It was at this time I went to Brisbane to do the Al Gore Climate Reality training. I was one of many hundreds being trained to be a Climate Reality Leader. My employer supported me on that. I still have that little badge. I got to see Al Gore and get trained by him.

I was still teaching at one university, but now I also started at another, teaching sustainability to post-grads. The post was close to where I worked at the aged care company, so it was easy for me. I'd landed the new gig via a lady I'd met during my very first job after my PhD. She'd overseen a project I'd run and, although we'd fallen out of touch, she obviously recalled me.

A new CEO came in at the aged care company, a lady from within the industry, and I was warned that she was a shark, a smiling assassin. Apparently, she loved me. Whenever I bumped into her she'd tell me, "Oh, Kaushik, I'm all about sustainability!" I talked her into joining a steering committee.

After I did the Al Gore training, I dove into an initiative that was going to boost my credentials. Climate Reality has a dashboard on their website where you can log in and, once you're signed up, you can add to your experience in the sustainability space. As part of the course I did, once you get the certification, Al Gore wanted you to go out and present to other people, and when you presented, you could log that as a credit on the dashboard. It's like a leader board kind of thing. And I love a good leader board, but I don't know why. Perhaps it's leftover from my tennis days!

Anyway, I started doing all these presentations at various universities, even to my body corporate. I started logging in all these things. One day I was lying in bed after having woken up early, and decided to check the Sustainability Reality social media accounts. I saw this post which read, "Project consultants needed for a forestry project in Perth. If interested, just message me." I quickly messaged her and she said, "Oh, thank you. I've passed your details onto this guy who lives in Tokyo."

Not very long afterwards, the guy from Tokyo rang me and asked if I was really interested in their project. He also asked about my background in forestry (which, of course, I did not have). Guess what I did? I completely winged it. I don't know what I said, but I gathered from our conversation that he was looking for an entrepreneurial/ innovation type experience. So I slipped in my experience of coaching start-ups at the university level. That worked a treat. Always be ready to leverage your experience. I can't stress that enough. The following will provide you with the tools you need in order to make full use of your experience, whatever that may be, to date.

Lesson 17: How Do You Leverage?

It All Comes Down to Who You Are

Begin by defining your professional identity. Who are you and what do you represent to the world? What are your strongest skills? Your assets? It's necessary to define this to know your value in the market.

Make a list of 10-15 of your accomplishments. Look at the common themes that run through your list. Every interviewer is going to say, "Tell me about yourself." Knowing your professional identity will help you create your elevator pitch for yourself. Be able to say who you are and what you do in one simple, compelling statement. This is your conversation starter about *you*.

Value Your Past Experiences

Don't downplay all that you've accomplished. Leverage your past experiences to get you to the next place you want to be in your career.

What is Professional Fulfilment?

Find your purpose. Think about where you can make an impact. All of my career advice leads up to this seminal goal. Your professional identity + values alignment = professional fulfilment!

How to Bounce Back (Continued)

The project was run by a Japanese conglomerate that had money and a piece of land in Western Australia. They wanted to gift this land to a start-up that could use it to create positive impacts on climate. It was like a competition. So I winged it. I knew the university coaching I'd done would be right up his alley. After a long chat he said, "Let me get back to you."

Two weeks later he said, "You're in the project team. So it's you, a guy from France and a girl from Mexico. It's all paid. You're going to get X amount of money. We're going to fly you to WA in March. You'll inspect the land, you'll understand it. Then you'll come to Tokyo for three days, we'll do a workshop on developing up this competition, and that's it, then you go back to your home country. We run the competition, and if you're interested in being a judge, we'll pay you for that as well."

Not long after I landed the job in Japan (it was only a side hustle, and wouldn't take me away from my work in aged care), my wife and I went to Machu Picchu and Easter Island. If you were to ask me, in all my travels to over fifty countries, all the experiences I've had in my life, what's the one place that's nearest and dearest to my heart? I would have to say Easter Island. That is the place that I would retire to if I could. Alas, my wife won't let me!

Honestly, it brought tears to my eyes: the moai statues, the remoteness of the place, the history. The people were beautiful. We hired an ATV and drove around looking at these statues. It just killed me, in a beautiful way.

Veema loved Machu Picchu. She loved the people of Cusco. They were very friendly. In fact, I was very sick the day we landed in Santiago. I had a fever of 101.3°F. Next morning, we flew to Cusco. Again, I was so sick. We landed in Cusco and had to drive two hours to the resort before going to Machu Picchu the next day.

Caption: Veema and I in Macchu Picchu

I was so sick, but I always find an inner strength. My parents say, "You've got an inner strength where when you're sick. No matter what, you just don't let people know; you just hold it in." I was close to passing out. I couldn't keep my eyes open on that two-hour bus ride from Cusco airport to the resort. I told Veema, "I need to sleep. Just let me be." I slept, and the next day I was fine. Veema and I are the best travel buddies. We've been to so many countries together.

Late in 2019, we went to Vietnam and Cambodia. If you ask Veema today what her most memorable trip was, it's Vietnam and Cambodia. It was a three-week trip with a group, a random group we met, a bunch of elderly people and us. We did everything from the Mekong to Cu Chi tunnels to Angkor Wat.

Caption: Halong Bay

We also had a very weird New Year's Eve party in Cambodia. It was a forced New Year's Eve party, so we didn't have an option. "You've got to go to this event," they told us, "You have to go to this event. You can't just roam around Siem Riep because you might get robbed." All things considered, we had a great trip.

When 2019 was coming to an end, I thought 2020 was going to be the year in which I was going to be unstoppable. Truth to tell, I was, but in a completely different spectrum. I thought, "My work is going amazingly well. And I've just landed Japan." I also wanted some global exposure. "I've just landed a new university gig. I've got the trip of a lifetime." I was telling Veema, "I want to go to Pyongyang, North Korea, in August 2020," because it was the 75th anniversary of the People's Liberation Army.

I'm fascinated by quirky places. I'd planned North Korea for August. I was going to go to Tokyo in April. Veema and I had also booked a trip to Singapore in December 2020. And in between we'd go to India. My employer was great about it; they would always let me go as long as I got my work done.

Work was going so well. The media were praising us. I thought nothing could stop us, nothing could stop me. That is a weakness of mine, no question. Every time I feel like I'm invincible, reality checks in. But this time it was about to check in for the entire planet.

I returned from the trip of a lifetime, and then it was January 2020 all of a sudden. I had one of my steering committee meetings in January. We had a project to roll out bamboo toothbrushes. A teenager in Queensland was making it happen. We were collaborating with this teenager to get bamboo toothbrushes into all aged care homes. We were doing some really quirky, strategic stuff, such as looking at waste contracts. It was all really good. I was lined up to speak at some big conferences representing my company.

February came along. That's when I told my employer, "I'm going to go to Tokyo for a week. Is that okay?" They were, of course, happy for me to get this experience.

It was also around this time I began teaching at a private business school that had a campus in Docklands, which was literally right next to our house. I'd been hounding them for a while about possible openings. Eventually, I think they got tired of me asking, so I was put in touch with the head of the department. She told me that she knew who I was, and that she'd heard about me from a lot of people.

She said, "I'm not even going to interview you. I'm going to ask you, what do you want to teach? You can teach whatever you want." I asked her what courses were available and we ended up settling on Corporate Governance on Monday and Tuesday nights. Now, that was a hell of a workload because Monday and Tuesday nights would be the business school, Wednesday nights would be university, and my aged care job full-time, plus Japan in the mix. People thought I was mad!

But that wasn't the end of it. Just before we'd left for Vietnam and Cambodia, tired of waiting to hear back from the business school, I sent out a bunch of similar emails to other private universities offering my services. One was the largest online MBA school in the country. So I sent a random email to them to their generic email address not long before our planned holiday. Before long, a response came back: "Can we have an interview?"

They asked me plenty of questions I didn't have the answers to. But I winged it. They said, "Okay. What would you like to teach?" I said, "Maybe Corporate Governance," even though I didn't know anything about corporate governance. And they said, "Okay. We'll come back to you."

When it rains, it pours. For some reason, whenever I go on holidays, things start to happen. Within three weeks of coming back from Cambodia and Vietnam, the business school reached out. Not long after that, the online MBA school came back and said, "We want you to teach Corporate Governance, starting in June."

So I'd just signed two contracts. I didn't worry about it. I don't think like that. I just do it and then figure out later *how* I am going to do it. Veema was saying to me, "How are you going to manage all this? You're going to be tired."

I was confident I could make it all work. There is a big difference between saying you're busy and saying you're efficient and productive. I very much dislike it when people tell me they're busy. The word "busy" doesn't belong in your vocabulary, because you can be busy sitting around looking annoyed, or you can be efficient getting shit done. I'm all for efficiency.

February came and I hadn't started teaching yet. The business school was set to begin in March. University started in March. And the online MBA school wouldn't be starting until June.

Then COVID hit and everything went up in smoke.

My trip to Japan was scheduled for literally a week after the world went into lockdown. That was the end of that trip.

At this time, too, my dad was in very poor health. In the months leading up to the COVID outbreak, he'd been in and out of the ICU a couple of times. As a child, my dad had terrible trouble with his liver. The doctors hadn't given him long to live. My grandma basically carried him in her arms to various people. They found a witch doctor, an herbalist. He gave my father some magic potion that kept him alive. These days, he's got diabetes. He has to inject insulin. And his kidneys are on the way out now too.

I had a trip booked to India in April so I could see my family for Easter. I was looking forward to seeing them; I needed to put a smile on my dad's face, and my mum was feeling very frail as well.

When COVID hit in March, our office went into lockdown. Everything was up in the air; no one knew what the outcome would be. The Japan people were determined to make the project happen; they were working out how to take it all online. Meanwhile, I packed up my office and started working from home.

The worst news was that, come April, I couldn't go to India. I was very disappointed, as were my parents. Work was very quiet. I wasn't getting very many emails. I wasn't sure what was going on. I called my boss's boss a couple of times, and at one point he said, "I think we all need to start looking for other jobs." He said he was joking, but there was something in his tone that wasn't quite right.

And then we ran a campaign called Hashtag Grateful Together. I was asked to do a video, just a 60-second video about how we're all part of the community, we want to do the right thing, we need to stay safe, what we're grateful for, etc.

We used to have these weekly catch-ups for a waste working group. My boss said, "Just cancel it, man. People are a bit tied up with COVID, trying to get PPEs and a whole bunch of things together. They're too distracted. Just call it a day."

Then the last week of April came along. I had a Zoom meeting with my bosses who told me that things were not looking at all good. They were having to let people go. Apparently, I had three options: Option A: look on the company's website and if there was another role, apply for it; Option B: put in a business case on why my role was relevant; or Option C: take the package they were offering and walk.

It caught me completely off guard, to say the least. I was living in another world. I thought I was too important to be let go, naïve as I was. Sometimes I'm just oblivious. I certainly didn't see that one coming.

I didn't panic. I didn't get angry. I didn't get upset. I just processed it. The plane was crashing and yet I remained calm. Veema panicked. She was asking me, "What are we going to do?" I didn't think about any of that. I didn't think about my family, I didn't think about life, none of that. I was just processing the information and thinking, "What's my plan of attack? What's the best move here?"

I then spoke privately with my boss's boss, who'd been on the Zoom call. He told me that 35% of the head office was going to be made redundant. He had to get rid of 75% of the property team because the company couldn't build anything for the foreseeable future. He told me he was sorry, but didn't know if he could save my job.

I said, "Okay. Now you're giving me three options. So if you were me, what would you do?"

He said, "If I was you, I would take the package. Option two is not viable. You can try putting in a business case and you can say these things, send it to me and I'll send it to the team that's reviewing, and I'm telling you they're going to reject it. But it's up to you."

I tried sending the letter outlining my value to the company. It didn't go through. I was left with little choice but to take the package and walk away.

I told my wife that it was game over. She was, of course, deeply upset. But I told her, "It's okay. Don't worry."

I sent off a farewell email to everyone, and received calls from people in tears, people were ringing me left, right and centre. I kept all the emails I got in response. I got feedback from 800 people across the business saying, "The business has made a huge mistake," and I kept it because I knew they'd made a mistake. But it was okay; I would move on.

I was at home. I said to Veema, "Give me a moment." She closed my door and I wept. I wept like there was no tomorrow, which is part of my therapy. That's just my way. I hold everything in for a long time. All the ups and downs go by, one after the other, and I don't react, don't react, don't react. But then something will happen and the floodgates open, and the open in a big way. It's just the way I am, my process.

The positive I took away from it all was that I had done my job so well that all my initiatives were now embedded across the entire business. The program was clear; the strategy was clear. One of things that I always used to say when I used to mentor people was, "I'll actually feel really good if my role is made redundant one day because I know that I've embedded things across the business." I didn't ever expect to be made redundant when I said that, but at the aged care company, I found closure in the fact of my legacy. Normally what takes 10 years took us two years.

The CEO told me, "You're going to go on to bigger and better things." Perhaps the biggest problem was that I'd done my job too quickly. It was like my PhD. I don't waste time. I don't sit around thinking about changing the world. I focus on something, a tiny dot, and get it done. That's the key: to focus on a single point, and get it done. I know had to train my skills, all my positive thinking, focus all my previous experience and gather together every bit of leverage I could find, in order to take my professional life in a new direction and pivot my career.

Lesson 18: Pivoting Your Career

"How people treat you is their Karma; how you react is yours."

– Wayne Dyer

The Benefits of a Good Mentor

I am not a full-time academic and I do not intend to be at this stage; I currently split my time between consulting, advising start-ups and academia, all while looking for that next amazing corporate role! With any luck, my next career pivot in about 10 years will be into coaching, mentoring and speaking on the development of sustainable, socially aware and profitable businesses.

As I look back, an informal pattern has emerged in how I orchestrated various career pivots in my professional life. Along the way, I've been fortunate to have great mentors whose advice at key moments performed miraculous reversals in my thinking. I hope that sharing this advice will help others successfully navigate their next professional chapter.

Keep Your Eye on Your Ball

I recently caught up with a well-known sustainability industry expert. As we chatted, he asked about my career and I explained my ambitions but was struggling to decide between various opportunities. What he said next was like the proverbial bolt of lightning: "Kaushik, you're going to fit into a lot of people's plans. The only question that matters is whether or not they fit into yours." Right there and then, the penny dropped. I realized that being crystal-clear in my criteria and priorities was the only way I would avoid getting sloshed around by every conversation or distracted by the next shiny opportunity that came my way. In short, keep your eye on your ball, not on all the opportunities out there that others might have in mind for you.

Lean Your Ladder Against the Right Wall

What you do with the talent you've been given should, and will, be largely determined by you and you alone. Gone are the days of working for a single company that outlines an enriching and varied career for you spanning the next three decades. As we move further into the gig economy, the ability to determine your own career path becomes an essential professional skill. Before you climb, be sure your ladder is leaning against the right wall. The best way to do that is to get your fundamentals right, be crystal-clear in your thinking, deliberate in your networking, and ensure you have the right mindset and framing to make the decision.

Understand Your Transferable Skills

These are the skills you've gained throughout our career. In addition to your job, these skills can also come from your volunteer work, hobbies, sports, and other life experiences. They can be used in your next job/career without any further refinement. They are transferable from one job to another. Think of a transferable skill as riding a bicycle. No matter what position you apply for, if the ability to ride a bike is a requirement and you know how to ride a bike, that is a transferable skill. In business, transferable skills can be things such as managing people, reading a profit and loss statement or knowledge of Lean.

Know Your Strengths

Understanding your strengths is another factor in your ability to make a successful career pivot. Knowing what drives you, what makes you "tick" is critical to the career pivot. Your strengths, once known, may lead you to an entirely different place than where you are today. For example, one of my greatest strengths is being a creative problem solver. I would not want to pivot into a role that does not allow me to use this strength. Keep in mind, that often your strengths are also transferable skills; I can be a creative problem solver in any industry, job or career. However, if I don't know that I'm a creative problem solver to begin with, I might be more likely to change careers rather than pivot.

Understand Your Personal Brand

Whether you realize it or not, you have a reputation within your personal and professional lives. That reputation combined with your strengths is your personal brand. Understanding your personal brand is the ultimate way to make a successful career pivot. More than just your appearance, your personal brand conveys to others who you are, what are you known for and how you add value to any situation. To really understand your personal brand, it requires self-reflection and a good deal of effort on your part. However, there is no other more important personal development process one can engage in, than discovering your personal brand. Knowing who you are, how you operate, and in a sense, what makes you tick will not only help you make a successful career pivot but it will also ensure that you pivot in the right direction.

Believe in Yourself

Change always involves risk, fear, discomfort and uncertainty, but navigating it successfully depends on one thing: believing in yourself. When it comes to changing your life, knowing that something better awaits you and believing that you deserve it isn't half the battle. It's the entire war.

One of the key things is to embrace change and invest in yourself. So be prepared to continue investing in yourself, whether that's a course or training, developing your skills, and maintaining your contacts.

Changing course can feel overwhelming, but it can be done. All you need are clear short and long-term goals and a roadmap to get there. As Jack Welch once said, "Control your own destiny or someone else will." There's never a bad time to make a successful career pivot. Life and work will be different once the storm passes. By following these strategies, you'll be prepared for whatever the future holds.

Lesson 19: Thrive in a Crisis

An Opportunity Rather Than an Ending

Never waste the opportunity of a good crisis. Redundancy can be a shock, particularly when it's the first time. Remember, you are not alone, and it should not reflect badly on you as many companies have cut staffing numbers in recent months. So first things first:

1. Don't panic
2. Take a day or two to take stock
3. Think, and
4. Plan your next steps.

It's easy to be angry when made redundant, but I recommend looking forward to a brighter future rather than holding onto one negative experience. In every experience, there is an opportunity to learn something. Even the worst setbacks can empower you.

For me, being made redundant has been a catalyst for something that can be truly wonderful. Losing a job allows us to reflect on our own lives and ask: "Am I genuinely living the way I want to?"

Current circumstances have pushed me outside my comfort zone, encouraged me to chase my next dream, reconnect with old contacts/friends and take on new frontiers. These were things I didn't do in a routine-based environment.

Charting Your Own Course

The biggest mistake a person can make is being afraid of making one. Most people need guarantees because they fear the unknown and uncertainties. Some people perceive going down an unexpected or different career path as a failure. They assert that their fate is predetermined and that they can do little to change their unfortunate circumstances.

Change requires courage; not everyone can take this leap of faith. Changing your career requires an optimistic attitude. Results require patience, and along the way, you may doubt yourself and your decisions. This is normal. However, by adopting a "woe-is-me" attitude, many people remain in an unhealthy state-of-mind that make them unhappy. Their self-doubt and fear prevail over their good intentions. I adhere to the following mantra to facilitate the change process in my thinking and behaviour:

Reality Plus Response Equals Result

You can't always control what happens to you, but you can control how you respond. Have faith and confidence that you can rely on yourself to get through turbulent times. Life happens, and everyone needs a break from time-to-time. So, press pause today and get yourself back on track when you feel ready.

Revenge

I was already plotting my revenge; not revenge on anyone in particular, but rather I was looking for a way to come out the other side of this disappointment in better shape than I was before it.

That Friday, I took Veema to dinner. I said, "All right. First, calm down, it's okay. Let's put things in perspective. We're going through COVID. People are dying. Whether it's because of COVID or not, people have always been dying of various issues. There's mental health issues. There's poverty issues. Now, put things in perspective. Do we have a home? Yes. Have we paid off your mortgage? Yes. Do we have teaching on the side? Yes. So, technically, we earn enough to have a mini holiday, good food on the table and live a comfortable life. Is that so bad?" And then she said, "Actually, that's not that bad."

I had three teaching posts, which meant I had a safety net. Overnight, my side hustle became my main hustle. I always had a plan B, without thinking that plan A would fail.

I hadn't told my parents yet that I'd been made redundant, because I knew how devastating it was going to be for them. Also, my dad was still sick at the time. He was in and out of the hospital. My mum was not well either. I was debating whether or not to tell them, but I have this tendency, as an only child, sometimes to tell them the worst and not really elaborate on the best. It's a strange thing. I don't celebrate my successes with them, but when something is terrible, I make sure they know about it.

Eventually, I decided to tell them. Saturday was the cleansing day, the detox day. I called them up and told them the bad news, and of course they were very worried. I didn't want to worry them, but I also felt that they should know. I tend not to talk to them every day, maybe twice per week is the most I'll speak with them. But obviously this required its own call.

I called them on Saturday. I told them straight. I tried to keep to exactly what happened, how it happened, how quick it was, how cold it was, the way it abruptly came to an end. Mum being my mum, she just started crying.

Dad being my dad, when you give him a challenge, it gives him life. So he woke up, put on his CEO hat, and said, "So, where to from here?" instead of panicking, he sprang into action. But he knew who he was talking to because that was the time he said, "I know you. And if I know you, you're probably already planning something."

But deep down, I hadn't really planned anything; it was all hyperbole. It was just in my head that I was plotting my revenge. I didn't have anything scripted, but my analytical brain would start doing that at some point. So I told my dad, "Yeah, I've got a plan." I didn't have a plan. I just said it to give them comfort. Maybe I said it to myself for comfort too.

The Rocket

I looked over our finances. We had until October. It was actually August, but I fudged some numbers and made it October because it sounded better when I told Veema. Anyway, I needed to get cracking.

I'm very methodical. I have a spreadsheet of contacts. This is probably common sense for many people, salespeople for example. But, for me, I had a different approach where I had a spreadsheet of names and companies. It was dynamic. I had locations, but I also had a column for helpfulness, how they had helped me in the past, how I had helped them. I had a column about whether or not I could lean on them. It was basically a relationship ledger.

Monday morning came around and I woke up, opened the spreadsheet and got to work. I had about 500 names in front of me, people who I could lean on, people I didn't need to waste my time on, people I needed to get in touch with. It was all done. So it's the hard work done over the years that didn't need me to scramble at that time.

I was also very strategic in my farewell email, because not only did I have one farewell email for the aged care stakeholders, I had an external stakeholder farewell email for people to know that I was in the job market. It was very strategically worded because I knew that would bring some feedback.

I built a plan of attack: Which colours were I going after? Was it the green colours who were ready to strike? Was it the ambers where I'm not sure, or was it the reds that I'm not going to touch but actually work in amazing companies? So what I decided to do was just actually go through the list and do maybe 20 names a day.

I'd never chased sales or business development. I did a bit of that when I was coaching in tennis, which might have helped somewhat. I had a template, a go-to.

By now my Japan project had kicked off and we were all doing it remotely. We were not going to go to Perth, we were not going to go to Japan. We were going to try and develop the competition virtually. So that was a revenue stream as well.

When reaching out to many people, I didn't ask them for a job straight off. In many cases, I asked for their advice on dealing with redundancies. It was more about, "Tell me your story. Did you go through something like this? How did you cope? What sort of feedback would you have for me?" Even though I was in such a vulnerable situation, I was listening to them, asking about them. People were receptive. There were collaborative conversations. People probably knew my intentions, but the approach was very critical in getting what I wanted. If your approach is poor, you might be the best person in the world, but you've likely lost half the battle.

So my approach was never one of panic or desperation. It was never one of looking actively for a job. I was simply strategic.

My outplacement specialist said to me, "You're one of the calmest people I've ever spoken to who's been made redundant." I said, "Oh, why is that?" He said, "It's just your approach." He was quite helpful in one respect, gave me a very good piece of advice. I'd sent him my resumé and covering letter, just to get some feedback on it. In response he said, "When someone reads your resumé and cover letter, they want to know your value proposition. You should include three bullet points of a value proposition on page one of your resumé." I'd never done that before. I hadn't even thought of that. I thought you simply included your experience, education, achievements, and so on and so forth.

That was a lovely nugget of information. And that's just the way to go about it. You don't go in wanting to change the world; you want to get a little nugget from one hundred different people, and slowly you'll build up a wealth of knowledge.

At this time, one of my university contacts asked if I would run an African entrepreneur program. There was an option to teach a master class on sustainability. And the pay was decent. So I pencilled it in for October. This was directly from my spreadsheet, a conversation with one of my contacts, who was a green.

Random things started coming out of the woodwork. There was a guy I'd mentored when I was teaching the start-up program. We caught up and he said, "Can you be on my board of advisors? For free." I said, "Yeah, why not?" So I met him for a coffee around June of 2020.

I asked him if he could promote it on LinkedIn. He did, and within a day I had someone on the phone who'd seen my experience and was asking if I could MC a start-up event. Then I received a LinkedIn connection from the CEO of an aged care company in Queensland, a not-for-profit, who was asking if we could have a chat the following week. He basically gave me my first major consulting gig. He wanted me to come in and build a sustainability program for them.

I asked him, "How did you find me?"

"I read your sustainability report and saw your name on it," he said. It is important to include your name on things like reports, for this very reason. It's not standard practice, but my employer at the time was happy to do it for me.

Every day during this time, I was scouring this spreadsheet, setting up Zoom meetings. I met very few people in person; most of my interactions were via Zoom.

I built the proposal, and in the meantime I had a thought. It was related to the way I'd approached my PhD, having to try and find around 40 businesses who would allow me to come and in analyse their sustainability performance. I could do a similar thing now. I said to myself, "I'm not the Kaushik that I was in 2011. I'm a much better Kaushik. A much more recognized Kaushik. So, what if I drafted an email, which I'll call a rocket? And what if I sent 300 rockets to the ASX300 companies, in particular to the chairpersons and CEOs of these companies?"

So that's what I did. In that email I said, "This is who I am, this is what I've done, this is what I'm looking for, and if you're interested, give me a call."

Initially, I'd sent it to the co-founder of a travel business whom I knew very well. I said, "I'm planning to send this rocket up. What do you think?" He gave me a couple of edits, and said, "Yeah. Looks good to me."

I also sent it to my friend in the outplacement specialist company, and I said, "What do you think?" He gave me some feedback as well.

So I built another spreadsheet: ASX300 company names, chairperson names, CEO names. I did my research, found their email addresses, or guessed them, and then sent up my 300 rockets. There was one thing I included in the email that might come as a surprise. In each case I wrote, "I'm a shareholder in your company."

Technically, I wasn't lying. There was a fund I invested in at the time, and this fund invested in all ASX300 companies. So perhaps it was a bit of a white lie, but it wasn't fabricated out of thin air. My email was more from that sustainability angle, from the perspective of an ethical investor. But it wasn't about pointing a finger; it took the tone of, "This is where I could add value."

To be honest, I didn't expect much. I could probably hope for maybe 30 responses, which might lead to 10 phone calls, out of which five might be interested, two shortlisted and one converted. That's the best-case scenario I could hope for. But I had nothing to lose, so I sent up the rockets. I was trying to stay positive as best as I could. But there were moments of bleakness, for sure. Veema and I had a big argument during that time, and thank God, till now it has been our last.

But afterwards I fell into a hole. I felt that I'd survived bullying and isolation. I'd drawn on the strength I got from that phase of my life, from all the tough situations I've faced. And now COVID had come, and with it a concoction of just about everything that was near and dear to my heart slowly started crumbling. My parents were sick. My wife hated me. The job through which I found a sense of self-worth threw me out. There was a time when I thought, "What's the point of all this?" There were shades of that bullying time when I was in my early teens.

Following the argument with my wife, I'd taken myself for a walk by the river. And at that moment, as I was sitting by the water in Docklands at about 8 p.m., feeling a little bit cold, I thought to myself, "This is petty. What's going on between my wife and I is really petty. It shouldn't be happening. I am just a number to the aged care people and I will always be a number to any corporation. I've got to accept that fact. My parents are an ocean away from me. They're not in my control. So, what can I do? I can't do anything about it." There was only one thing within my control, that little dot I could hone in on. That's what was most important, because my marriage was the only thing I could really do something about.

So I took myself home and we sorted things out. And, you know what, after that we became much closer. It was a marriage lesson: tough times can break a person or relationship, but they can also make them. The redundancy and COVID brought us together. We tell the whole world, "COVID saved our marriage, it didn't break our marriage," because we became so close, because my mindset, my vocabulary, my thinking, my dealing with Veema's pressures; I've learned who she is and I've learned who I am.

Still, I didn't have any leads. I didn't have a full-time job. I was just kind of floating. But if I had an ounce of entrepreneurial blood in me, I would have known to make something out of this. I could have been an MC; I could have been a master class guy. But that just wasn't me.

Soon the replies started coming in from some senior people from some well-known companies. Some wanted a phone chat, some politely declined my offer, saying the team was already set, and some were saying, "Maybe you could be a consultant for us." Of course, there was also the standard, "If something opens up, we will let you know," and, "Something might be opening up in the near future." I received a diverse range of responses. As expected, the number was around 30 to 40.

I had nothing concrete at this stage, and so I told my wife, "We haven't gone on a holiday for a while. Why don't we go to Bright?" We'd always wanted to go to Bright. It's just a very beautiful place. Very tranquil. I'm not a tranquil kind of holiday person, but we had to make the best of our situation. Veema agreed. Pyongyang was our preferred option, but that was out of the question now.

So we went to Bright, which is surrounded by mountains. It was very beautiful. We stayed next to a river. There was something about the situation and the environment. It was all just connecting really well.

And lo and behold, I got a call! Once again. It always starts with that call when I'm on a holiday. I got a call on day two.

The way we travel is, I always plan the day; we wake up really early, we go for a trip, come back, and then Veema needs to take a nap. She tires easily in the sun. And then in the evenings we go out for dinner, and that's pretty much it for the day.

Veema was in the middle of a nap at around 1 p.m. when I got the call. I picked it up. The voice on the other end said, "Hey, this is so-and-so from XYZ company." Now, by this time I had lost the plot in terms of which companies I'd emailed and which ones had responded. I didn't know what was going on. It's just my nature.

I spoke to this person and I was pretty much winging it, as per usual, because I didn't have my spreadsheet with me and I couldn't remember who was who and what was what. We spoke about sustainability and salary and expectations—the usual things.

In the end, he said he'd get back to me. Something he said struck me, and so I asked him if he could send me the position description. They'd been trying to fill the role they'd called me about for some time and hadn't been able to find anyone. I thought it might have something to do with how they were selling it. What I didn't realize, was that the position was a composite of two roles. One job, two hats.

Around this time I'd submitted a proposal to the not-for-profit who were being sluggish. They were umming and ahing and, to be honest, they were turning me off. I was concerned that they were wasting my time; I'd put in a fair bit of time in building that proposal.

Soon enough, the other company called me back and requested an interview. And then, within minutes of concluding that call, another company called. Within an hour of that one, the next company called. All in all, I had four who were keen to talk; much more than I'd expected. Added to this were several firms who wanted me on a consulting basis.

While all this was going on, I built my own website and started to blog about health and wellbeing and those sorts of topics because I felt that was good material at that time, especially around COVID. I thought, "Let's try and make a bit of a diversion from what I usually write about, which is climate and sustainability."

That website, it became my brand. I didn't build it for that. I just built it to be a repository. But, in essence, it was my online, living resumé, which people could refer to whenever they received a rocket. They'd tell me, "You've got such a good website. You've got a LinkedIn profile. How come you're still on the market?" It was very beautiful to hear.

All of a sudden I started getting calls for roles in Europe, post-COVID, or Queensland or Perth. One was a mining company, one was a food company, one was an education provider, one was in healthcare. So, again, it was quite diverse in terms of the interests.

The not-for-profit was still on the side. I was in a conundrum there. Should that come through, it was going to be a big gig that I might miss out on if I landed a full-time job. But the timing was important to get right. If I declined one and the other one became a "No," or if both became a "Yes", it could make things tricky. There were a lot of permutations in the back of my mind. I didn't know where I was going with any of it.

Anyway, I did the interview with the mining company. Of course, it was done via Zoom. I couldn't see the people on the other end of the line; for some reason their camera was not working. I don't know if that was a lie or not, whether the camera actually was not working or they didn't want me to see them. Maybe they were trying to test me. I don't know.

So we had a chat, and I completely forgot what the role was about. I'd done no preparation, nothing. I should have, but I didn't. They even said to me, "You know the company's based in Sydney, right?" To which I replied, "Oh, yes, I know." I didn't know that. I didn't know I'd have to move. Veema wouldn't have let me send that rocket out if we had known. They asked me if we'd be open to moving, and I told them, "Yes, of course!"

In the end, the person on the other end of the call (who I'd still not seen) said, "You can't see us but if you could, you would notice that I'm writing handwritten notes and passing them to my colleague every few minutes." I said, "What does that mean?" She said, "You're good and we want to take you to the next step."

At this point, I vaguely remembered they'd been trying to hire for this role but I didn't ask any questions around, "Why couldn't you find anyone? What's the issue with the role? Complexities? Is it the company culture?" Nothing. I just went with the flow.

They told me that the next step was a six-hour leadership assessment. A test for six hours! I thought, "Oh, God!" I'd done half-an-hour or an hour written or psychometrics, but nothing like this. They told me not to panic, which I didn't; I was more worried it would be a drag more than anything. Still, I told them I was up for it.

Within a couple of days, the not-for-profit people come back and say, "We're ready to accept your proposal for the job, for the piece of work." I had to call and be frank with them. I mentioned that they were dragging the chain, and in the meantime I was interviewing for another role. I said to him, "Can you park that thought?" He was fine with that.

This was all happening, of course, during Melbourne's lockdown of June/July 2020. Melbourne was one of the worst hit by COVID and consequently one of the early cities to go into an extended lockdown. Life was bleak. We were living in a 69-square-metre apartment, so it was cramped, to say the least.

I did the six-hour test. It was basically a leadership simulation with real people that popped up on the screen in all different sorts of scenarios. There was also a written component. One of which, for example, required me to read a case study within 15 minutes and then produce a spreadsheet to analyse the data, pull together a PowerPoint presentation, and then actually present it to a real person after 30 minutes. There was a lady on the other end assessing my performance.

I must admit, I prepared a bit for this one. I called the CIO of a former employer a week before and asked if he'd ever done anything like a six-hour assessment. He said, "The max I've done is four hours. I had a four-hour test to become a CIO."

I did the test on a Tuesday, and by Thursday they were on the phone with me with yet more questions and another, "We'll come back to you."

I politely asked them to let me know by the next day. I needed to know, because the not-for-profit opportunity was hanging by a thread. I didn't want to lose both. On Friday, they called and made me offer, one I couldn't refuse. And that was the company I work for today. That's how I landed the job. It took a lot of juggling and hoping for the best; a lot of sending out rockets and talking and nurturing relationships—but in the end it paid off. Undoubtedly, at times it was nerve-wracking, but on the whole I remained calm, as I always do, even in the direst of situations. I just have an inner stillness, I think, a sort of knowledge that things will work out.

Winging It

The offer from the mining company was almost too good to be true; certainly one I couldn't refuse, even if it meant moving to Sydney. But it was a big step for me, and Veema was on-board with the move. I was going into new territory, still within sustainability but now I was in the mining industry. I didn't know a great deal about that, didn't know the unspoken, inherent values of the industry. But I wasn't nervous or apprehensive. I knew I would take it in stride, and I'd find my way through it.

I started my new role in August 2020, which meant I needed to wrap up all of my teaching. This wasn't a mandate from my new employer, but I thought it was important so I could dedicate myself fully to the business.

If you look at how my career had progressed, I never jumped into the same role at another firm; there have always been changes and evolutions. At the aged care company, it was more or less change management, but with a bit of environment and energy sustainability programmes, via which I rolled out like four gigawatts of solar energy across the country, 25,000 LED lights, and waste programs. My role before that was very environment-dominant, though I'd also weigh in on things to do with overarching strategy and change management.

My current role complements my preceding roles; now I focus on the social aspect of sustainability. I asked my boss, "Sum up my role in two words," and she said, "stakeholder engagement." So, the first hat that I wear is social responsibility.

The second hat that I wear is investor relations from an Environment, Social, Governance (ESG) perspective. Many investment companies are coming after corporates around emissions, carbon footprints, human rights, etc.—basically any breach of corporate responsibility. My role is to be the intermediary. We have a Head of Investor

Relations who looks after the entire investor relations piece, while my job is drilling down into the sustainability aspect of investor relations.

The third hat I wear is ESG reporting. ESG has exploded since COVID hit. Ever since the world has become focussed on health and wellbeing (even more so than before COVID), investors—institutional investors, pension funds—are all basically saying, "Okay, corporations, what's your ESG performance?"

Sustainability is a holistic concept; it holds businesses accountable. Whereas ESG makes their efforts more measurable. So it's one thing to tell us, "I have a sustainability strategy," but if you don't actually *measure* and *monitor* those impacts, how do you know if it's working?

ESG reporting is basically storytelling; it's telling the story of the great work we do across the business and across our sites in terms of sustainability. People read the report and they say, "Okay. You're a company that's worth investing in." It's basically a dossier of the ways in which we are managing the issues society deems important.

Hitting the Dots

Whenever I walk into a new company, I establish three dots I'd like to hit. In previous roles, I've had juniors ask me what my aims were. After gaining some experience with the company I was with at the time, I had an idea of the targets I wanted to hit. And so I told my colleague: "I've got three dots that I want to hit in this company. The first dot being, I want to embed sustainability across the business." Now, the whole leadership team and the board were nervous about this, and that came largely from their not understanding it. But if I could do a good job of building a strategy and taking care of the change management, it would ease them into the waters; it would introduce them to certain ways of thinking, new ideas and protocols that will make them more aware and less frightened of these changes that will happen whether they like it or not. It was just the way the world was going. So my first dot was to make the company feel comfortable about the future from a sustainability perspective.

"The second dot I have," I said to my junior, "is to make the company an industry leader in sustainability." I was sure that with the programmes I was implementing and the awards we were landing, I could make a name for us on the sustainability front.

My third dot was more personal, but related to the other two. Primarily it was to build my brand, through the business. While boosting the company's reputation, I could simultaneously boost my own. It was a win-win. I was sure to keep all of my personal online resources up to date with each new initiative, award, conference, and speaking opportunity. As we forged ahead, others came to attribute my name with the good things that were happening in the sphere of ESG.

Those were my three dots. I wasn't aiming to change the world, just three areas that were within my reach. I could make these happen. It wasn't pie-in-the-sky thinking. One of the most important things when setting goals is that, while you need ambition, they need to be reasonable and achievable. Otherwise you run the risk of being quickly disheartened.

Veema: Part 2

Veema and I have grown closer together since our wedding. At first, when we met, I was transitioning from being a spoiled brat into a mature adult. Perhaps I was still on the brat side of the transition! But, in those early months, I stayed around. Which was new for me. I'm an only child, and I've always walked away from relationships. Up to that point, I'd learned to survive on my own; I was self-sufficient, so I could easily walk away from a relationship, a job, a friendship, anything. If something wasn't panning out as I'd hoped, I could just move on, just like that. So, for me to have stuck around, that was very weird.

I was transitioning into being a fully functioning adult when we first met. So there were, I admit, a few bumps in the road. Ultimately, though, I think she's the reason I've transitioned to a more empathetic person, to someone who can place themselves in another's shoes.

Veema and I are madly in love. When we were on stage at our reception in India, my dad's siblings said to me, "Kaushik, you've met your match in Veema because you're very childish and so is she." The whole time on stage we were giggling together, and that's how we are today. I know until the day we die we're going to be the way we were when we first met. We're going to hold hands, we're going to kiss. We're going to be cute. We're going to be stupid. We're going to be immature. And we love it. We love that about our life. I think that's what got us through, but, boy, things got rockier after that wedding. It got very rocky.

Veema is the most important person in my life; she's taught me a lot of life lessons. But to get me to learn those lessons, we had to return from a very, very dark place.

After returning from India, we moved into an apartment in Docklands. We had planned a honeymoon trip to Las Vegas and New York. It had always been my dream to get married by Elvis Presley in a drive-through wedding chapel. Just for fun. Which would make it four weddings it total: our paper wedding in Melbourne, then Mauritius, India, then Las Vegas!

We went to Las Vegas and Veema just fell in love with the place, all the glitz and the lights and everything. We saw a couple of shows.

But the wedding itself was the highlight. An Elvis impersonator sang to us. There was, of course, a real pastor on hand. We basically renewed our vows, because obviously we were already married. Veema was walked down the aisle by Elvis! She was infatuated with him. She didn't really recognize me at all! I was beside the point.

But she does say, of all the weddings, that was when she felt like she was truly getting married to me because it was so serene, so quaint, it was so beautiful. And that said a lot, you know? Like, in Mauritius, she wore like 20 kilograms of gold. But that's not her, not really. Jewellery is not her; fanfare is not her. She is fairly reclusive, introverted. And so, she loved that wedding in Vegas. That was the time she said, "I'm getting married to you and I love it!"

That was our fourth wedding. After Vegas, we went to New York. Veema hated New York, hated the big city, which was the complete opposite to what we'd just come from. Lots of chaos. Lots of dodgy areas. We saw an NFL game, but had to leave at halftime. Veema didn't like the sport, and when she doesn't like something, it's very hard to keep her going. There was an explosion about that, which lasted a couple of days. That was probably the scar of the honeymoon. Otherwise, we had a good time. But every time there was a scar, it had something to do with her past, not that I realized this at the time.

We returned to Melbourne, where we bought our apartment in Docklands. During these times, our arguments were huge. I'd try to keep a lid on things, but as they grew and grew inside me, it would get to the point where I'd have to explode. And at some point, I started getting Veema's parents involved. I just couldn't take it because she's just a very complex organism. I needed help managing her temper and her feelings and sensitivities. You've got to be very, very patient. You've got to compromise a lot. And even then, it may not work out.

At that time, her dad was alive. She was very attached to him. He could connect with her and help with her state of mind. But even then it was hard, because he wasn't well. Still, I spoke with him and he told me, "I'll talk to her." Unfortunately, not long after that he passed away, an event that was obviously terrible for all of us. With him gone, so too was my male confidant who could help me understand Veema. He helped me to feel that I wasn't alone.

When we lived in Faulkner, he gave me some essential advice. One day, when she had left for work, I was at home with her parents who were visiting. The subject of Veema came up and he said, "I just need to give you one piece of advice. My daughter is a handful. So, you need to pretend like you have water in your mouth, because when you have water in your mouth, you can't talk. And that's just how you got to do it."

Things have been very turbulent at times. Even her mum said to us one day, "If you guys argue one more time, you need to separate. You need to divorce." That's how bad it got.

Travelling is what brought us closer. I'd never travelled the world before, except for tennis. Veema asked me, "How come you didn't travel so much when you were single?" And I said, "I was more social. I liked to get drunk and party. But I knew the day would come when I'd find someone special and we would explore the world together."

When we travel, I'm the orchestrator. Veema just comes along for the ride. That's just how we work. When we went to Tasmania, if you'd asked her where she was going in Tasmania next week, she wouldn't know the names of the cities we would be visiting.

I make a plan and she says, "Yep, whatever. I'll follow you." She leaves it to me.

A couple of years ago, just before I started working at the aged care company, we took a six-week holiday to India, Mauritius, Jordan and Egypt. It was a wonderful trip. We were on a group tour. Veema just loved it. We met 20 other people and had some of the best times in our lives, the tour, sailing along the Nile in a boat. She always says, "You had many girlfriends. You've travelled the world. You've been independent. Whereas I've always been protected. I haven't really travelled. I've had lots of issues as a kid. I've never known how to deal with it. I've never had a boyfriend. So, this is all too much."

Caption: Jumping over the Pyramids in Egypt

Caption: Love Easter Island

Caption: Petra in Jordan

Caption: Angkor Wat

Caption: Macchu Picchu

While we were in Mauritius, I wanted to stay in a resort for two nights, even though her family lives there. If you go to Mauritius, you've got to stay in a resort; that's a bucket list thing to do. It was actually at this resort that I got that call from Netherlands offering me the Amsterdam gig, which I went on to decline.

The night before that, they had what was called a sculpting tour. It seemed interesting, so we signed up for it. We sat down, the guy gave us some clay, and said, "I want you to sculpt a dodo bird." Of course, the dodo is the national bird in Mauritius.

Now, I don't profess to being the most skilled in the area of sculpture, especially the sculpting of birds. Which is to say that my dodo came out something like a zombie bird—a zombie bird that was severely disabled.

But when Veema made hers we all stopped and stared. The guy taking the class asked, "Have you sculpted before?" She'd never done it in her life. But it was incredible. I'd never even suspected this side of her.

When we were on the plane back to Melbourne, I asked her, "Tell me about your artistic side." As a child, she loved art. She wanted to be an artist. But, of course, her Indian parents were against it. No, she had to be a doctor or a lawyer or a businessperson. So she studied chemistry in the end, and hated it, which is why she hated school and detests study in general. I never knew about her interest in art before; it not only opened up a dimension within our marriage, it also promised a way forward in terms of a vocation for Veema.

But after we returned from that trip, the arguments started up again. My professional life was going really nicely, but my private life was a real struggle. Even though everything was lovey-dovey and we were travelling the world and we'd been together for a few years, I was still ready to walk away. Even today, I'm ready to walk away from anyone, not just my wife. Anyone, at all. Veema says to me, "That's very weird about you. You have no sense of attachment to anything."

Of course, not long after we got married, the subject of having kids came into the equation. Our families were beginning to apply the usual pressure: "When are you going to have a child? You bought a house; when are you going to have a child?" Sometimes I feel more like a project to my parents than a living, breathing human. The assumptions of many parents is: you're born, do high school, get a degree, get an MBA, get married, buy a house, have kids, become grandparents, and then you die. That's how it feels, especially for an Indian child.

That pressure was behind some of the biggest arguments I had with my parents at the time. I knew Veema was stressed about it. But I told my family, "Guys, this is my view of the world. You live once. I live once. I've got one stakeholder that's very important to me, that's my wife. So, if we have a baby, which she doesn't want, how is that going to make my life? And if I die, am I going to take anything with me? No. So, just give us some space. And if we don't have kids, we don't have kids. And if we want kids, that's up to us."

Meanwhile, Veema's artistic side was simmering away beneath the surface. One day, about 18 months after we came back from our trip which involved the sculpture tour, she said to me, "Can I get some polymer clay and just start making some designs, some artwork?" I said, "Of course, do whatever you like."

So, she ordered some clay and some tools. She started making things, small things, testing designs: fridge magnets, for example. They were tremendous.

I also think not working was playing on her mind, so when she started making things, it helped her to feel productive. I always encouraged her in it. Really, I didn't mind if she worked or not; I just wanted her to do whatever made her happy. But she seemed to enjoy it, and it was very therapeutic.

After she made the dodo bird in Mauritius, she told me, "When I was working on it, I felt something. I felt something I haven't felt in decades, and that was peace and calm and tranquillity." And I thought, "Okay, this might be the magic thing, just to get her to do this. And that'll hopefully help her."

Also, she was going to therapy at the time. I don't really believe in therapy and I questioned her on it. She told me that she needed it, and that she was going with or without my blessing. I was really upset, and argued with her. When, really, I should have taken my father-in-law's advice and pretended to have water in my mouth and said nothing. I should have just let her do what she needed to do. But I made a big deal out of it. And she just left me in Melbourne. She took a Skybus to the airport and flew to Mauritius. I think my parents were coming to see me at the time.

I felt like that was the final straw. I was ready to walk away. But she came back—her family had a two-year memorial of her father's passing—and we'd both cooled off. We planned another trip; this was when we visited Easter Island and Machu Picchu, a very moving experience for me.

It was around this time that I realized I needed to be more relaxed in our relationship. To hold the water in my mouth and let Veema do what she needs to do. It's for the benefit of everyone, not just her and me, but our families as well.

But late 2019, Veema took her clay work to a consignment shop where she could display her artwork, and promote her wares. Then we applied to get her a stall at the Docklands markets. She hated actually selling her works, so I manned the stall. I was the one peddling her wares!

Veema started with a deodorant for the market, for which her sister had given her the recipe. She made a first batch of 10. We were the most amateur stall-holders. We had a foldable little table with a tablecloth. We didn't have any equipment, no signage, nothing. We just printed something on an A4 paper, put 10 deodorant boxes on the table. But, you know what, I sold all 10 by the end of the day! And we lived next door. So, we just packed up our table. We finished two hours before the end of the market. From the outset, our entrepreneurial endeavour seemed very promising.

Very soon her collection was growing. It included key chains, earrings, bookmarks, candle holders, and more. It was time to start getting things happening for real. Initially her shop was called Creative Crafter. To begin with, sales were slow, we did a bit better than breakeven. And then, 2020 came around.

In May, we established an Etsy shop. We also changed the company name to Klay Creations. We chopped and changed things quite a bit around this time. But ultimately I said to her, "You've got to stick to a plan. Otherwise you won't find momentum." Soon she started getting orders from around the world.

Now we've established Klay Creations as a small business. The income isn't huge, but it's doing quite well. On the other hand, with the value of nurturing Veema's passion and its overall impact on her on a human, this venture is priceless. It puts a smile on her face. It makes her sane, it keeps her calm. And she just loves it. She says that she's found her calling, which is absolutely wonderful. And at the same time, I've learned that she needs to be allowed to do what she needs to do. I've taken my natural inclination to go with the flow and applied it to my marriage.

The biggest lesson Veema has taught me is how to succeed in a relationship, in a marriage. Honestly, if there was a marriage that was going to fail, ours would have been it. To begin with, it was a recipe for disaster. Things turned extreme between us at one point, and we've come back from the edge of it all crumbling away. Our parents have told us, "This is like a soap opera." But we've both learned things about ourselves and about each other. And now we're like glue.

In the end, she taught me how to deal with conflict. And now I take that into the workplace. I'm very good at conflict resolution. Today, I'd give my life for Veema. Would I have six years ago? I don't know. But now, yeah, I would. And it has nothing to do with COVID or being stuck at home together. She has taught me to allow for and accept people's differences. That it's very rare that you're going to be on the same page as someone else. If you are going to have any sort of relationship with a person—romantic, marital, professional, friendship—you have to realize that there *will* be differences.

I have the ability to turn my life around completely, if I need to. When you don't have an ego, and when you're not bound by anything, it's amazing what you can do for yourself. I'm always willing to give things a go. Even if it means changing my entire mindset just to make someone happy. It's hard to do. It's not easy. But sometimes it's worth doing it.

It's a lot like climate change and sustainability. All the data supporting it is out there. There are facts regarding the need to act more sustainably. Companies just need to be willing to make that change, one step at a time, in order to save the world. We need to show them that a mindset change will not only benefit the planet, but will benefit them as well. There just needs to be the will.

I have a will. It's my invisible sword, and I can just wave it when I want, if I want to do things that others say are not possible. Also, I don't mind failure. It's something you have to be prepared to accept. I seriously don't mind failing. It doesn't bother me. It happens, and you always learn from it.

At work, I tell my team, "If it fails, it's okay, guys. You've done a hell of a job." And I am always mindful to tell the core team that, "You guys have done a great job. If anything happens, I'm going to take the fall for this, so don't worry." One thing that's often missing in big companies is accountability. Whereas, I'm the complete opposite to that. I will take the hit for anything because it's not that big a deal to me to take a hit. Okay, I get a hit. I can handle it.

In the end, a lot of that mindset has come from my relationship with Veema. I've learned that I can handle much more than I thought I could. I've also learned that things need to take their natural course, so you need patience. Often the best thing to do, particularly in relationships, is to do nothing—let things work themselves out. They always do. That's the thing that Veema has taught me, and it's something I apply to everything, everywhere, be it work, life, or relationships.

Conclusion

Saving My Father's Life

It was around the time the world went into lockdown that my father was in very poor health and taken to the ICU. He'd been unwell for a while, but things were not looking good. Still, initially I was happy to let Mum take care of him until I visited at Easter. But with the lockdown looking like it was going to be extended, who knew how all that was going to work out?

Whereas someone else, like my wife for example, would want to race off to her parents' side, I'm different. I wanted to go back, but I also didn't want to go back. Not because I didn't want to see them, I did. It's something of a weird psychology I have about showing affection. I think we've always been at arm's length when it comes to affection. We love each other dearly, but we're not overly big on displays of affection.

I asked my mum, "Do you want me to come?" She told me she'd take care of it. Veema was telling me, "You probably should go. It might be the last time." But I wanted to let things unfold. I was always compartmentalizing. When I went to work, or when I was in a Zoom meeting, I would switch off.

But at that time, I'd wake up, check my WhatsApp, and think, "Is he dead today?" I had to check manually because I always switch off notifications. If I want to know what people are doing, I'll go and check their profile, which is probably why I get such a good sleep. Even my own parents, I muted their messages to me in this WhatsApp group because sometimes it's just a bit much and I can't be bothered.

The downside of that is when I wake up, I might have missed something critical unless they called me. One morning, I saw 10 missed calls from my mum. So I immediately called and Mum said, "I'm in the ICU. Dad's gone back in." His sodium level completely dropped, he lost control of his body. He didn't know where he was. It wasn't looking good.

But Mum was adamant I should stay in Australia; she'd look after him. For them, my career was very important; they don't want to get in the way of it, even when something dreadful is happening.

At that time, my routine involved starting the day with a WhatsApp message, working till about 5 p.m., and then calling Mum for an hour, then back to my wife, and then with my mum again. Everything was up and down, it was so intense. Dad's body was failing him in so many ways. It was just horrible

At the same time, COVID was rolling through the hospitals in India. We were worried that Mum might catch it because she never went home. She would just sit with her mask on a bench outside the ICU. She's fiercely loyal to him. She'd already had COVID in June, which didn't hit her that badly surprisingly.

But that first time he was in the ICU, he rallied and we were all relieved. But there was some sort of lingering infection, and within a couple of weeks he deteriorated rapidly again. His organs were failing. The doctor himself couldn't figure out what was wrong, and then at some point, for the first time they called an ambulance. They raced him in, and I was totally oblivious. The next morning, I saw all those missed calls. Mum called and said, "This time it's not looking too good, Kaushik." And I said "Okay. Don't worry about my job, just focus on Dad." For me, the issue was not the job. When it's time, it's time. Everything else is irrelevant.

The main reason I was triggered into going was Veema. We were having a coffee that afternoon because I was working from home. Veema said, "You have to go." Initially I was hesitant, and said, "Maybe I won't go this time, let's go in April because by then COVID will be over and done with. We can celebrate Easter, we will both visit. It will be nice." Clearly, I was living in a fantasy world. But she said, "No, you should go. The way things are panning out with your dad, I think you have to go."

I called my boss and said, "I have to go to India. I'm happy to resign. Would you like me to resign?" I didn't even think about asking if we could negotiate some time off. I felt it was disrespectful. I've had lots to do; I didn't want to just push it aside, because then it piles up and affects the team. I didn't want that, so I offered to resign so someone could take over my job. But my boss was great; she said she wouldn't accept my resignation. She told me to go and do what I needed to do.

Of course, there was the pandemic and related restrictions to consider. I had to get a letter from the hospital explaining Dad's condition. Mum got hold of the letter for me, and I applied for leave very quickly. Even better, within six hours I had my approval.

At that time, Melbourne was coming out of COVID lockdown, and there weren't many flights. But there were heaps from Sydney. Basically, I took a calculated risk. I had a team meeting scheduled in Sydney. So, I thought, "Here's a chance to get to know my team." I'd actually never been to Sydney to see my team. I could do that and then get on one of the few flights out of the country.

So off I went to Sydney, where I met my boss and my team for the first time. I remained cheerful and managed to compartmentalize. I found I could focus on the things I needed to focus on, without my worries about my family overwhelming me. For now, I kept them behind a locked door. I could inch forward on the issues I was dealing with at the office, going from room to room in my mind. Nobody could tell my dad was in dire straits, and I was about to go on this trip.

I spent a few days in Sydney, and then at the team dinner I received a text from my agent. My flight to India had been cancelled. I had to wait in Sydney until a flight opened up.

The team dinner was on a Thursday night and it was looking like I'd have to wait until at least Monday for a flight. I called my travel agent and said, "I need a flight. I don't care what happens, I need a flight." She told me she'd try to work something out. About half an hour later, she calls me back and says I could get out on Saturday night with Emirates, but I'd need a negative COVID test. Trouble was, COVID tests needed to be done 48 hours beforehand, and it took 24 hours to get the result. Nevertheless, I said, "Don't worry, I'll figure this out on my end. You just book me on that flight!"

Despite everything that was going on, I ended up working the whole of Friday. Work came first; it was just like my dad, that's how he was. Even if he was dying, or there were family issues, he would go to work; the personal stuff would always wait.

Obviously, I needed to get a COVID test on the Friday so that the results would be in by Saturday.

The paperwork was a nightmare. I needed to do one set of paperwork just for the Indian government, and then I needed to do another set of paperwork for the Tamil Nadu government, which is the state government. I checked into my new hotel, sat down and got to work.

Next morning, Saturday, I went into the pathology lab at 8 a.m.; I was the first person there. I told the nurse that I had a flight I absolutely had to make that night, was there anything she could do for me? She was wonderful. She said she'd try to help me out. And within three hours I got my test result. It was a miracle.

Eventually, I got to Sydney airport. It was so sad. It was completely empty. There was a salad bar that was open but completely deserted, apart from the son and father manning the counter. They looked at me with dead eyes. It was only one of two restaurants open. I bought three salads, two yoghurts, and a couple of drinks just to see if I could do something for their small business. I couldn't eat most of it, but I did buy whatever I could. The effects of COVID were very clear to see.

It was even worse when I arrived at Dubai, which was usually a busy, hustling, bustling airport. It was just dead, like Las Vegas with nobody around.

Eventually, I arrived in Chennai and made my way to the hospital. A few days prior, they'd moved Dad out of the ICU. Nevertheless, I wasn't prepared for what I was about to see. I hadn't processed how he was going to look.

It was around 3 a.m. and technically I was supposed to go into home quarantine. But I didn't mind going to jail; I had to see my father. Besides, this was India, and rules can be bent here.

I arrived at the hospital, went up three flights of stairs, and walked to my father's room. Bear in mind that up until now, I've seen my dad as a very charismatic, strong CEO; a very humorous and restless guy, very strong-willed, who likes to go out, likes to make jokes, likes to have fun, and was a little bit strict. Which is to say, he's always been full of life and also imperious. I'd never seen him weak. When I did see him then, it came as a shock. Everything was shifting, my family life, my work life, and I had to harness a strong mindset in order to deal with the apparent uncertainty of the ground beneath my feet. I needed something of a paradigm shift in order to cope with the mounting stress.

Lesson 20: Shifting Paradigms

Reactive to Proactive

Shifting this paradigm means taking control of your stress instead of reacting to it. You can't avoid stress, but you can minimize it. For example, proactive people avoid having to worry about their finances by saving money and following a budget. They also exercise, eat well and get regular check-ups to ease their stress about their health. They avoid relationship problems by being respectful, kind and forgiving. Research shows that a lack of control builds a sense of stress, while having a sense of control, lessens anxieties.

Unmotivated to Inspired

If you're not enthusiastic about your job, your lack of drive could provoke stress or be a reaction to stress. The antidote to being unmotivated is to get inspired. Create a mission statement that compels you. List your values. Rank them from most to least important. Write about each aspect of your work that relates to your values, principles or ideas. Rephrase each value into a positive clarifying paragraph, a series of present tense, first-person declarations, such as: "I am healthy and strong, I treat myself with respect and manage my stress in excellent ways." Consider these purposeful statements as you make choices all day; put every decision, no matter how small, through that filter. Using your values to shape your actions decreases stress.

Pressure to Priorities

Many people feel overworked. They cope with pressure by "multitasking"—trying to do several things at the same time. But no one can truly multitask because the human brain can focus on only one thing at a time. Trying to multitask actually causes more stress. When you attempt several tasks simultaneously, none of them get your full focus and attention. Instead, shift your paradigm from pressure to priorities by scheduling what you need to do, one thing at a time. List two or three of the most important steps you need to accomplish in a day, and forget the rest for that day. When you write out your priorities, you will feel less stress about trying to "do it all".

Hassle to Harmony

Everyday workplace annoyances may include turf wars, territoriality, ego issues and plain old fear, being afraid of not moving up, or not getting a contract, or just fear of "losing" out in general. Instead of thinking of life as a battle with a winner and a loser, consider how both sides can win. For example, the retail giant Costco carries a variety of goods, offers customers a generous return policy and pays employees well. Some retail executives might think these policies pose a risk of losing money, but Costco knows how to keep its customers loyal. And, by paying good salaries, it minimizes turnover and saves them money in the long run.

Anxiety to Empathy

To manage anxiety, be more empathetic. Empathy is not sympathy. Empathy is understanding what others feel. Sympathy is feeling sorry for others and comforting them. Practice empathy by listening to people with the intent of understanding them rather than listening to respond. Although technology makes it easier to communicate, you may be having fewer face-to-face interactions; that can increase social anxiety. Empathy declines when people isolate themselves. They hesitate to invest emotionally in others and don't realize how isolation generates stress.

Empathy requires mindfulness, focussing on the present—a major tactic in stress relief. Consider what you're seeing, hearing, tasting, smelling, touching or thinking at this moment. Like exercising your physical muscles, building mindfulness becomes easier with time. Try this exercise: Go to your favourite restaurant alone, and relish the experience. Instead of eating quickly, savour each bite of a dish you love. Focus on how each spoonful tastes as you eat it.

Defensive to Diverse

Feeling defensive often leads to "job strain". Constantly guarding your territory can exhaust you and shut you off from different viewpoints. For example, Blockbuster maintained a defensive stance when Netflix founder Reed Hastings approached company leaders about working with his firm, which offered video rentals without hefty late fees. Blockbuster declined his offer and went bankrupt, while Netflix flourished. Such organizational "group think"—or even stubborn adherence to a popular, single point of view—can lead to missed opportunities and lost profits. Challenge defensiveness by being open to diversity. Welcome different kinds of people, opinions and attitudes. Be open to travel, especially to places where you've never been.

Dad

A word here about my father and the impact he's had on me. When I was a child, my dad inherited a job in Lagos, which was why we moved there in the first place. The company wasn't at its best at the time, but over a period of 30 years, he built it into a global, multinational corporation. He became the managing director for Africa and was more or less the reason that the company survived and became what it is today.

Caption: hanging out with Dad in Hyderabad

Growing up, I wasn't a great student at school, but I was an excellent observer. I would love spending time with my parents, especially when the conversation was nice and friendly and so on and so forth.

In terms of his work, I was quite close to his colleagues, at least the Nigerian colleagues. He would take my mum and me to functions, and I would watch all of them look up to him. It fascinated me. It seemed so strange for people to be in awe of someone who was just my dad.

Sometimes, he would yell at them and they listened. I'd think, "You're yelling at these people and they're doing your bidding. It's not very civil, and they're still civil to you. How does that even work? What's going on here? I'm scared when you yell."

As he became the managing director and the business gathered momentum, I continued watching him. He was so diligent. He'd wake up very early at a certain time. He would work, finish at 7 a.m., have breakfast, shower, and then go to office. He would come home, shower, have his tea, and then work again. He'd have dinner, and then he'd work again.

I remember overhearing telephone conversations in which someone would call and say, "Mr. Sridhar, your truck has been hijacked by kidnappers or armed thugs, and they're asking for a ransom in a briefcase." I heard that multiple times. My dad would never get flustered. He wouldn't be perturbed, he wouldn't be shaken. He handled those situations very calmly and deliberately. I think I absorbed that via some sort of osmosis.

Other times, there'd be calls where he just yelled. He would yell as though he was about to kill someone. But I also saw him being cool as a cucumber in some very high-pressure situations. I saw him making deals with people, and then he would tell us stories about how he's trying to influence stakeholders to make multimillion dollar deals in Nigeria, where corruption and bribery is rife.

In my younger years, I didn't look up to anyone. I didn't look up to my mum. I loved her, but I didn't look up to her. I was perhaps closer to Dad; I would lie next to him when we'd go to bed. So the only person that I started looking up to was him, and the reason I looked up to him was because I saw this very dynamic individual who seemed to be operating effectively in a high-stress, high-risk environment, who was able to get things done in a way that had multiple dimensions. He would yell, then he would be chilled. He would be very shrewd, very smart. Very soft, very hard.

I witnessed all these different aspects to him, and some things started to stick in me as well; not that I was conscious of it. Watching him and listening to him on those phone calls in my younger years went a long way in forming the person I am today, in forming the values I have now.

Sometimes I went to his office. As a treat, he took me there on the way to the tennis court. I sat in his big office, and people would come in and their hands would be shaking to get a signature from him. I'd see these people shaking, standing there right in front of him, and he would suddenly take on a different persona, more stern, more authoritative; but once the person left, he would be my father again, playful and cheeky and up for a good time, just like always.

I think I'm made of similar stuff. Veema says, "Kaushik, you have these personalities which are very annoying and hard to comprehend. You play with me like a kid, but then you get a call and you just become a different person, someone who we should be scared of. And then you have this other personality where you're trying to schmooze this person." I definitely got that from Dad. He took that company from near bankruptcy to a multi-billion dollar enterprise; he's obviously got the traits of a CEO. Learning from him was a very critical part of my journey.

Which means, I think, that often his anger was part of a role he was playing. He's naturally very soft, but he's got a side to him that, if it came out, anybody would be scared.

And I think I'm a bit like that; I rarely explode. Very, very rarely do I lose my temper at work. In fact, I've been told many time that I'm the jolly, smiling presence in the office. I don't think they'd believe Veema if she told them about my temper.

But even when I do lose my temper, it can be calculated; for sometimes it's important to be seen as angry. I know exactly what I'm doing, even when I argue with my wife or anyone; it's often about principles. If a line has been crossed, I will have to raise my voice and express my disappointment. I'll wait and wait, but once the line has been crossed, that's it. I'm careful to remain in control, because the moment I finish what I need to say, I go back to being a puppy dog! Again, I'm compartmentalizing.

Fairness is very important to me. I take a lot of shit, and some people think I can be very soft. Like even my boss, not long ago, she saw me speak to a consultant, and later on she called me and said, "Everyone thinks you're soft, that you leave yourself open to exploitation. But from what I've seen today, you're a smiling assassin."

I've also been called a friendly "badger". It's all about stakeholder engagement; it's a way of getting things done. Sometimes, I've got to hassle a lot of people to get on with it. I think my dad was very good at that, at pushing people to get the best out of them, to get them to keep going, and not become lethargic or lazy.

My dad was also very sensitive towards the way people from other cultures operated. He had to go to London, he had to go to Hong Kong. He had to go to many developed countries as part of expanding the company's operations. So he knew about cultural differences. When he took meetings with key investors or stakeholders in the developed world, he knew how to switch his personality and I would think, "Are you the same guy who was yelling all the time in Nigeria?"

My dad's versatility, his ability to manage people, to treat them in the most effective way, always with a view of creating what he set out to create, was hugely influential on me. As the years went by, I understood more and more just how good he was at what he did. I learned not only how he did it, but I also learned to appreciate it. I think that it's very important to have a mentor, which is why I take on that role for many people these days. In my early years, my dad was my mentor, maybe not officially, but I certainly watched him like a hawk. I absorbed everything, and it has stuck with me. Now, most of it is just muscle memory; I don't have to even think about it. It's just how I operate. But if I drill down into how I operate, and why I operate the way I do, a lot of it has to do with my father. I have so much to thank him for.

Coming Home

But now I was in Chennai, and I was making my way to the ward in which my gravely sick father was possibly dying. I went to the doorway and peered in. I was not ready to see him in this condition. He'd loomed so large in my imagination; he was an overwhelming presence in my life. And now here he was, with some 15 or so tubes going into him, sitting up in bed with a nurse next to him. The nurse said, "Hey, your son has come from Australia."

Dad looked at me. The funny thing was that he'd had a fall earlier in the year where he'd lost a tooth, and so when he smiled at me, there was with a huge gap in his front teeth. Anyway, he smiled and said, "Welcome to India!"

He looked so thin and frail and powerless, the opposite of what I was used to. It hit me like a sudden gale, this man who'd brought other grown men to tears, was now withered and drawn, and I had to excuse myself. I'd been putting it out of my mind all this time. I'd been focusing on work, on Veema, on anything other than Dad's condition. But when I saw him in that hospital bed looking like a ghost, it all had to come out. I knew it would crush him to see my reaction, so I left the room for a moment and had a good cry. This is just how I process these things. I cried and cried and cried. Then I tidied myself up and went back in.

I stayed there for six weeks. I cared for him like I've never cared for anyone before. We brought him home within a week. Then it was up to Mum and me. I did everything; I'd wipe his ass, I'd shower him, I'd feed him, I'd yell at him if he misbehaved, and I would be working in between. All the while, I was working.

I had to yell at him a lot because he was very naughty with his food. We had some massive arguments. Some people would say, "How can you yell at your dad like that when he's just come out of ICU?" But when I left he said, "You came, and saved my life." I asked him how he meant that, and he replied, "Firstly, with your presence. Secondly, your willingness to whip me because no one has had the nuts to do that!"

Caption: A happy and healthy couple once again

It's funny, because when I thought I might lose him, my affectionate side came out. I would play with his hair, I would give him a hug, I would give him a kiss on the cheek. This was a surprise to me, because we'd never been affectionate like that as a family before.

But it was touch-and-go for a while there. His liver was gone, he needed a liver transplant, but he couldn't have one because he was too frail. His kidneys had failed, he needed a kidney transplant as well, but that wasn't going to happen. His diabetes was out of control, as was his blood pressure, he had glaucoma, and on top of all that his feet were swollen from water retention.

So he had to be kept like a flower. He couldn't have any stress. I remember the last day, I'd never had this sort of conversation with them before, but at 37 I decided to be a grown up. I said, "You both need to sit here, and I'm going to give you some advice for the first time in my life." They'd been married for over 35 years, and they'd had a very turbulent relationship, which I'd seen with my own eyes. But that all had to stop. They had to now be gentle with each other. I couldn't come over and care for them at the drop of a hat. If they kept arguing, kept stressing each other out, they would be the cause of each other's deaths.

It was tough love, but I had to tell them straight. "Don't mess this up," I said, because I wanted to keep coming back and visiting them with Veema for the next 30 years. I had to be tough, otherwise my father wouldn't listen to me. For example, he couldn't eat chilli, but of course he loved chilli. He would try to sneak it. So one day, I told him that if he ate that chilli I was not going to eat at all. The decision was his. If he had that meal, I was not going to eat for the rest of the day.

I tried to keep a positive mindset. I told him, "You can be fine, you don't need to be like this. You can actually be fine, there's nothing wrong with you. You can actually be fine. You just need to calm down, and listen to Mum, and behave."

Even now, two weeks ago he was back in the ICU because he didn't behave. I found out exactly what happened. So for five months he listened to me, and then he lapsed back into old habits. And I was tough with him. I said, "Too bad. I told you what not to do, and you did it. So that's where you end up".

It was tough love, and that last night my mum was boiling. She was like, "How dare you talk to us like that!" But, I said, "Ma, you need to let me finish", and she actually listened to me, which was a first. So I said what I had to say without a temper. And for the most part, it all got through.

Then, with my father now in much better shape, it was time to leave. But while everything was settling down with my parents, things were about to take a turn. Getting back to Australia was a complete nightmare.

Once I'd decided that it was time to leave, I felt an urgency to get going. Firstly, a new strain of COVID had turned up in the UK and the global community was starting to panic. Countries reintroduced lockdowns and closed borders. Australia, lockdown capital of the world, placed increasing restrictions on international arrivals.

The other reason I wanted to get home was Veema. She'd been in Melbourne the entire time. Since getting married in 2014, we hadn't been apart for longer than a week. Added to this was the fact that I had a new job which required my attention. While I had worked most of the time I was in India (a much-needed distraction), my workstation was a laptop and a mouse, which was taking a toll on my physical health. The more I thought about it, the more I realized, at the very least, I needed to start thinking about a way back.

To begin with, I had a return trip booked for 16th January. But then I received news that my first flight back via Sri Lanka (on Sri Lankan Airlines) had been cancelled. They then cancelled the flight on 23rd January and stated that 1st February was the next available date (not that they were guaranteeing anything). Sri Lankan Airlines had stopped flying to India due to the UK mutant strain until 1st February. On top of this, apparently Sri Lankan Airlines wasn't flying into Australia for the time being. But on checking the FlightRadar app, I could they see were indeed flying into Australia. Something wasn't adding up. Perhaps, I thought, they weren't flying into India and used that as the reason to deter passengers from booking flights from India to Australia.

Meanwhile, I was furiously talking to my Australian and Indian travel agents, and both were struggling to find the silver bullet. One had me on a flight to Adelaide via Kuala Lumpur. I felt this wasn't a good option at the time and, boy, am I thankful, as Malaysia would soon announce a state of emergency and my efforts to get home would've ended then and there.

My local agent was feeding me information which was relatively unhelpful. Basically, I couldn't leave India and couldn't get into Australia as both countries were tough with their border restrictions. I knew the problem; I needed a solution.

Not quite at my wits end yet, I spoke to a friend of mine whose husband had just been to India and got back in relatively smooth fashion. The route he had taken: India–Maldives–Sri Lanka–Melbourne. High risk, but why not?

I jumped on the Sri Lankan Airlines website and there was one business class ticket (I found out later this was the last one) left for 15th January from the Maldives to Melbourne via Colombo. So, Sri Lankan Airlines *was* flying to Australia; they just weren't flying to India.

I decided to take a gamble and booked this flight. I then booked a local flight from Chennai to Mumbai and then to the Maldives for 14th January. I was more worried about the Maldives–Melbourne flights cancelling, and never expected anything unfortunate to happen with the local flight.

On 6th January, there came the dreaded news that the Chennai–Mumbai–Maldives route had been cancelled. I instantly thought of the Maldives as the COVID capital of the world; Malé wasn't coping at all well. I had a knot in my stomach as I thought all airlines from India might cancel flights to the Maldives. I checked the travel website and found another airline (the only other airline) going to the Maldives, via Bengaluru. I booked it instantly and kept my fingers crossed. If this flight got cancelled, all hope was lost!

I had never used the FlightRadar app as much as I did between the 6th-14th of January. It seemed like I was checking it every five minutes! Flights were being cancelled left, right and centre. I also noticed some Sri Lankan Airlines flights being cancelled; social media was alive with stories of the company's unreliability. Oh, and did I mention someone told me Sri Lankan wasn't flying to Australia? Sometimes, less information is less stress.

Despite all the negative and somewhat conflicting news, I kept my head down and stuck with the ticket. Every day, I jumped on a live chat with the airline to check flight status. So far, so good.

The day before my scheduled departure was 13th January. With a knot in my stomach, I checked the Sri Lankan Airlines website to ensure the flight immediately preceding mine was still scheduled to go ahead. This would give me solace that, if it was still going, then mine should be too. To my horror, it was cancelled!

I spoke to the airline and they gave me information which made no sense. I told my parents not to worry; if I got stranded in the Maldives or Colombo, I would figure out a Plan B. In true Kaushik fashion, when the stakes were high, I didn't have a backup plan.

On the morning of the 13th, I did the COVID test and once again, as per routine, filled out all paperwork relevant for the Maldives and Australian governments. I managed to complete and upload everything in the nick of time. At least now these countries were aware that Kaushik Sridhar was coming across their borders, and COVID-free as at 13th January, 10 a.m.!

It was now the morning of the 14th. Coincidentally, 14th January is the most important day in the Tamil calendar, which is when they celebrate the festival of Pongal. However, I had a flight to catch, much to my parents' sadness. Upon arriving at the airport at 3 a.m., I checked in for my flight to the Maldives. The check-in staff asked me if I had a visa for the Maldives, to which my response was, "I'll get it on arrival." Naturally, I had done zero research, but I had such confidence in my response that he said, "OK!"

After clearing immigration, I had a smooth flight to Bengaluru. Boy oh boy, did India take COVID travel seriously. We had to wear a face shield, mask, white coat, and use sanitizer. It was a requirement for all to wear and use. I don't even want to think about the waste being created from this pandemic!

Following my arrival into Bengaluru, the Silicon Valley of the East, I transferred to the International terminal, and once again, I had the airport nearly to myself. I took my scheduled flight to the Maldives where, upon arrival, I went straight to immigration. The officer raised a fuss about my not having a visa and while I tried to explain

I was only in transit, she was adamant that I could not leave the airport, let alone stay in transit as my flight to Melbourne was a different ticket.

My knight in shining armour was a male senior officer, who came to discuss my paperwork. Things were about to get very strange. With my hand on my heart, this is actually what happened.

The two immigration officers proceeded to have a rather flirtatious conversation right in front of me for several minutes. I mean it. While I stood there with my bags, trying to avert my gaze and detach myself from whatever was going on in front of me on the other side of the counter, he played with her hair and she kept touching his shirt. Things were getting pretty steamy! I just wanted to be allowed to stay in the airport until my flight came up.

Now, no doubt somewhat hot under her collar, the officer finally stamped my passport and let me in. This was the most bizarre experience I have encountered at a country's immigration point. We've all heard stories of people flirting with officials in order to get their own way, but how many times has another official stepped in and done the flirting on your behalf?! Very strange indeed!

Anyway, I got to spend the night in the Maldives. While this might sound glamorous, I stayed in Hulumale, a man-made island which wasn't so glamorous at all, and frankly, quite dead (except for the million coffee shops lined up along the one street; and I had a juice instead of a coffee just to be different).

On the morning of the 15th, I arrived back at the Maldives airport to depart, and had to go through a paperwork check before I could even enter the airport. They scanned a QR code that I had received upon uploading all my documents on their portal (my unique code to state I was COVID-free prior to arriving in the country). This was scanned when I arrived in the Maldives and I was wondering why they scanned it again. Letting it go, I then checked in, had a royal treatment for flying business class, and felt this was a sign of good things to come. Was I wrong!

I went back to immigration, and when the officer checked my paperwork (a different officer from the day before, thank God!), he asked for the QR code. I gave him the code and he said it was invalid. Apparently, I need *two* QR codes: one for arrival and one for departure. I asked what's the difference and he didn't respond. Instead, he told me to fill out the appropriate form and get the new QR code. This was much easier said than done. I didn't have Wi-Fi on my phone, and the airport Wi-Fi wasn't all that good. His response, "This is not our problem; please leave the airport, get the code and come back. Otherwise, you cannot leave the Maldives."

And so, I went back downstairs, took a breath and tried the Wi-Fi. It didn't work. I tried again. Nothing. I then went outside and, in between a Coffee Club and a car park, I found a signal! Excited, I logged in, went to the Maldives Health Declaration portal and filled out the lengthy form. It asked me to upload a photo on a white background. Now, anyone who has visited the Maldives will perhaps recall that it is all pink. Everywhere you turn something is painted a shade of pink. Where on earth was I going to find a white wall?

After plodding around for what seemed like an eternity, I finally found a patch of white. I ran to an airport staff member and asked him to come with me to that patch of wall so he could take a photo of my amazingly tired face. He smiled and knew what was going on (inside joke?) and took the money shot. I uploaded the photo, submitted the form and, boom, got the QR code. I ran back, looked the immigration officer in the eyes, and gave him the new QR code. I purposely removed my mask and showed him my smiling face. He smiled back and realized he had met his match.

After an hour in the lounge, I took the Sri Lankan Airlines flight from the Maldives to Colombo. It left 45 minutes early because they didn't want the local cleaners to come in and clean the aircraft; according to the airline, the cleaners from Malé might have been carrying COVID. That's how bad the situation was in Malé at the time.

Being the only passenger in business class (yes, I was the only passenger), I was given the royal treatment. The head attendant, Viveka, was very kind and we spoke for about 30 minutes regarding COVID, travel, vaccines, life during and post-COVID, and also her trials and tribulations as a flight attendant. She told me that she had travelled with 20 COVID-positive passengers from London (in March 2020) and didn't know this until they reached Shanghai. She couldn't hug her own daughter because of her profession. However, she didn't want to quit because she loved what she did. After loading me up with snacks and bottles of water, she bid me farewell as I disembarked in Colombo.

Rather than going to the gate or airport terminal, we were stuck in the airport bus for 30 minutes. The people whose job it was to disinfect the gate were running late. At last, as everyone was getting very agitated, they arrived and sprayed disinfectants on our bags, shoes (and my arm accidentally). We were then escorted to a gate with no lights or air conditioning. The entire airport was deserted, and we would be stuck at this gate for the next four hours because the Colombo–Melbourne flight was delayed by two hours.

But there was much more to it than that.

When I got into Sri Lanka, while at the airport, my body started to heat up. I wasn't sure if I had a fever or not, but it started heating up. I had the feeling that I was about to come down with something. With everything that was going on, I had a sinking feeling, to say the least.

My throat was starting to get a bit scratchy, I had a feeling I may be running a temperature, and my stomach was not right. We had to wait at the gate for four hours because the connecting flight from London was two hours late. All the while, I was starting to feel worse and worse.

At last, we boarded our flight. From Colombo, there were three of us in business class. My body was on fire, but I kept quiet. I sat like a stone pretending nothing was wrong with me. The air stewardess didn't have much work to do, so I was left alone. All of a sudden, I lost control of my bowels. It was terrible. I was feeling horribly feverish, weak, and then this. Not only was I feeling wretched, I had another 10 hours on the plane.

Whenever the air hostess happened by, all I could ask for was green tea. By about four hours into the flight, my clothing was no longer in the best shape. I had to figure something out because I didn't have a change with me. I had to get innovative, a bit creative with my jacket.

I just kept telling myself, "I've got to get through this. I've got to get through this." I didn't know what was wrong with me. I had a temperature and a sore throat and now an upset stomach. What if they didn't let me back into Australia. Could they send me back to Sri Lanka?

The air hostesses were coming through to check our temperatures every three hours or so. Each time they walked past me I thought I'd had it; they were going to chuck me out of the plane or something. And yet, despite feeling wretched and like I was overheating, my temperature was always normal.

At long last, we arrived in Melbourne. I still felt like I was going to explode; all I wanted to do was run for the toilet and get home. But we had to sit on the plane while a recorded message played from the Australian government about COVID. It went on for probably 10 minutes, but it felt like hours. All the while, I was thinking to myself, "Lady, just shut the fuck up because I need to get out, and get through this thing!"

Finally, they let us off. But, of course, then we had to navigate the checkpoints. They asked me: "Do you feel hot? Do you have diarrhoea? Do you have a cold? Do you have sore throat? Do you have any of these?"

I said, "Nope." I said no to everything. They checked my temperature, and it was normal. I got through. Then it was off to the SkyBus, which is parked under the plane. We had to wait another 45 minutes for the passengers from another flight.

How long had it been since we'd left Colombo? I couldn't bear to count. Anyway, eventually I got to my hotel to quarantine. The whole thing probably took a good four hours from the time the plane landed to getting into a room. I just sat in the room, and I thought, "How in hell did I just get through that?" When I was home and out of quarantine, I narrated this story to Veema, and she said, "If anyone could get through this, and lie through their teeth it would be you."

It's true, I have been through a lot. I have gotten myself through a lot. I've had to. I effectively left home at 13 to enter the tennis academy in Texas. I grew up sleeping next to my parents, and then one day all of that changed. I had to sleep alone. I had to stop wetting the bed. Overnight. I had to learn how to cope with being bullied, day in, day out. It's not something I'd wish on anyone, but I got a lot out of it. In a way, it made me who I am today, propelled me into the kind of work I do now. It also, with the assistance of my PhD supervisor, taught me that most of life is out of my control; if the plane's going down, there's not much you can do to stop it. The world is the way it is, and you will have only a very minor impact. On the vast white page of existence, you have only a tiny dot for territory. It's your job to find out what lies within that dot, to hone in on those things and set about impacting them. It might not change the world, it might not change anything, but it will be a contribution, and you will have a purpose and drive.

You can only affect what's in your immediate vicinity. What others do, how they feel about you, how they think–is all beyond your control. But within your dot, there are infinite possibilities to be creative and effective. This is where you can use your imagination and energy. I've come to thrive on problems, and even learn from failure—or, rather, to see failure as an opportunity. It's an opportunity to spin something else out of the threads of disappointment.

Coming home from India, despite my distress, I was okay. I had remained calm. My body was distressed, but inside, in my mind, I was dealing with it. I thought to myself, "Let's just see what happens." I didn't panic. I allowed things to unfold. That's key. Just like that day, all those years ago, while sitting aboard a plane to Texas with my mum and dad, en route to the tennis academy, when all of a sudden we started going down. I could do nothing about it then, and I could do nothing about my situation now. My tiny dot was my own distress; that was the only thing I could control. I had a quiet confidence that it would all be okay, that everything would work out. I just had to ride it out. I just had to wing it.

Caption: *"The Gate of Heaven", Lempuyang Temple, Bali*

Acknowledgements

Writing a book is harder than I thought and more rewarding than I could have ever imagined.

There are countless people I would like to thank for their help throughout my life, without whom I would not be who I am or doing what I do. For the sake of brevity here, I would like to acknowledge and thank those who have had the greatest impact on the success of this book.

I have to start by thanking my awesome wife and best friend, Veema. From reading early drafts to giving me advice on the cover, she was as important to this book getting done as I was. A lifelong partner makes both the journey and destination worthwhile.

I'm eternally grateful to my parents, who taught me discipline, tough love, manners, respect, and so much more that have helped me succeed in life. Without your unconditional support, this book never would have come to be.

I owe an enormous debt of gratitude to Geoff Manchester and Peter Bol who not only wrote my forewords but gave me detailed and constructive comments on one or more chapters. They gave freely of their time to discuss nuances of the text and pushed me to clarify concepts, explore particular facets of work, and explain the rationales for specific lessons.

Thanks to everyone else who played a significant role in helping this book come to be.

Manufactured by Amazon.ca
Bolton, ON